FOR ORGANS, PIANOS & ELECTRONIC KEYBOARDS

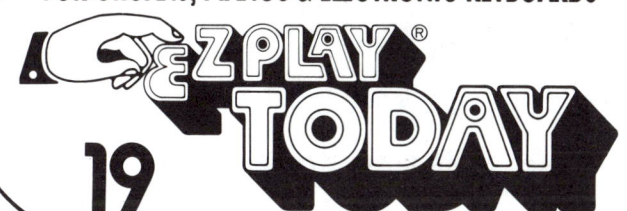

POLKA AND MARCH BEATS

Y0-EAL-086

THE KEYBOARD CENTER
100 W. Chicago Rd.
Sturgis, MI 49091
616-651-9232

E-Z does it! That's why E-Z Play TODAY Music was created. This series has been designed with a special music notation for instant playing enjoyment.

The collection of songs in each book has been specifically arranged for use with all major brand organs, including chord organs and those with automatic chord units. Special chord notation is also included for the triad and conventional chord player. The entire series provides a play-on-sight repertoire filled with musical fun for everyone . . . delightful tunes that will appeal to every musical interest.

Before you begin your "E-Z" adventure, read the next two pages for a "playing preview" of the special notation and a full explanation of the chord symbols used throughout the series. If this is your first encounter with organ music, you'll be able to enjoy instant playing fun. If you've had previous organ playing experience, you'll enjoy having a complete variety of music at your fingertips. In any case, there are hours of musical fun ahead for everyone.

Contents

- 2 Playing Preview
- 4 Barbara Polka
- 6 Can Can Polka
- 8 Clarinet Polka
- 10 Columbia, The Gem Of The Ocean
- 12 Friendly Fellows Polka
- 14 Helena Polka
- 16 High School Cadets
- 18 Julida Polka
- 20 King Cotton March
- 22 La-La-La Polka
- 24 La Sorella
- 26 Liberty Bell March
- 28 Lucia Polka
- 30 Mademoiselle From Armentiers
- 32 Martha Polka
- 34 Pizzicato Polka
- 36 Semper Fidelis
- 38 Sharpshooters March
- 40 Thunder And Blazes
- 42 Tinker Polka
- 44 Toreador Song
- 46 Guitar Chord Chart
- 48 Chord Speller Chart (Keyboard)

7777 W. BLUEMOUND RD. P.O. BOX 13819 MILWAUKEE, WI 53213

E-Z Play® TODAY Music Notation © 1975 HAL LEONARD PUBLISHING CORPORATION
© 1976 HAL LEONARD PUBLISHING CORPORATION
Made in U.S.A.   International Copyright Secured   All Rights Reserved

E-Z PLAY is a registered trademark of HAL LEONARD PUBLISHING CORPORATION.

Playing Preview

THE MELODY (Right Hand)

The melody of a song appears as large lettered notes on a staff. The letter name corresponds to a key on the keyboard of an organ.

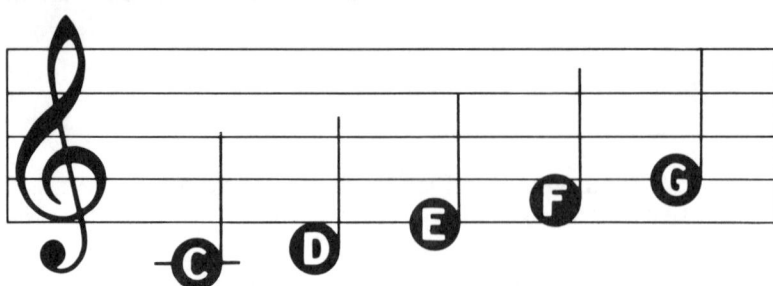

ACCOMPANIMENT (Left Hand)

The arrangements in this series have been written for all types of chord accompaniment.

1 One button (chord organ) or one-key chords.

2 Three-note (triad) chords.

3 Conventional, or standard chord positions.

Chord names, called chord symbols, appear above the melody line as either a boxed symbol [C]

or as an alternate chord (C7)

or both C7
         [C]

1 For chord organ or one-key chords, play whichever chord name is on your unit.

2 If you are playing triad chords, follow the boxed symbols. A triad chord is played like this:

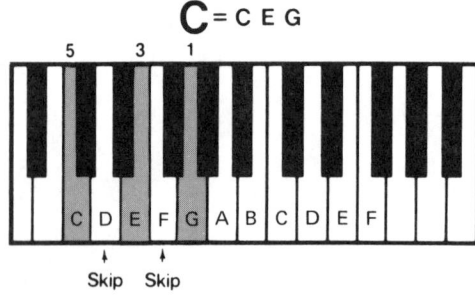

- Place your little finger on the key which has the same letter name as the chord.
- Skip a white key and place your middle finger on the next white key.
- Skip another white key and place your thumb on the next white key.

In some cases, there is an ARROW to the **left** or to the **right** of the chord name.

The arrow indicates moving one of the triad notes either to the **left** or to the **right** on the keyboard.

To understand this, first think of a chord symbol as having three sections, representing the three notes of the chord.

An ARROW is positioned next to the chord letter in one of these sections, indicating which of the three notes to change. For example:

- An arrow to the left means to move a note of the chord **down** (left) to the next adjacent key.

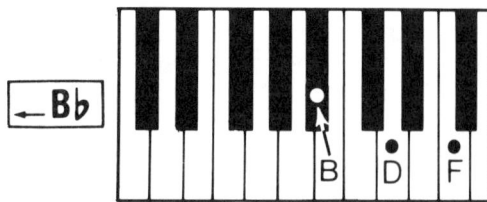

In this example where the arrow is in the **lower left,** or "1" position, move the first note "B" **down** to the black key B♭.

- An arrow to the right means to move a note of the chord **up** (right) to the next adjacent key.

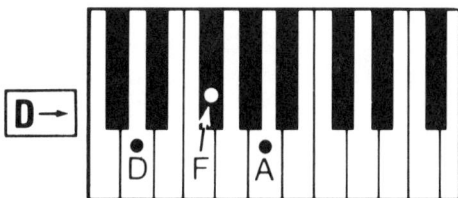

In this example where the arrow is in the **middle,** or "2" position, move the middle note **up** to the black key F♯.

3 If you are playing standard chord positions, play the chord in the boxed symbol, unless an alternate chord is indicated. Play alternate chords whenever possible.

For your reference, a Chord Speller Chart of standard chord positions appears in the back of this book.

REGISTRATION AND RHYTHM

A Registration number is shown above the music for each song. This number corresponds to the same number on the Registration Guide which appears on the inside front cover of this book. The Registration numbers also correspond to the numbers on the E-Z Play TODAY Registration Guides that are available for many brands of organs. See your organ dealer for the details.

You may wish to select your own favorite registration or perhaps experiment with different voice combinations. Then add an automatic rhythm...and HAVE FUN.

Barbara Polka

Registration 3

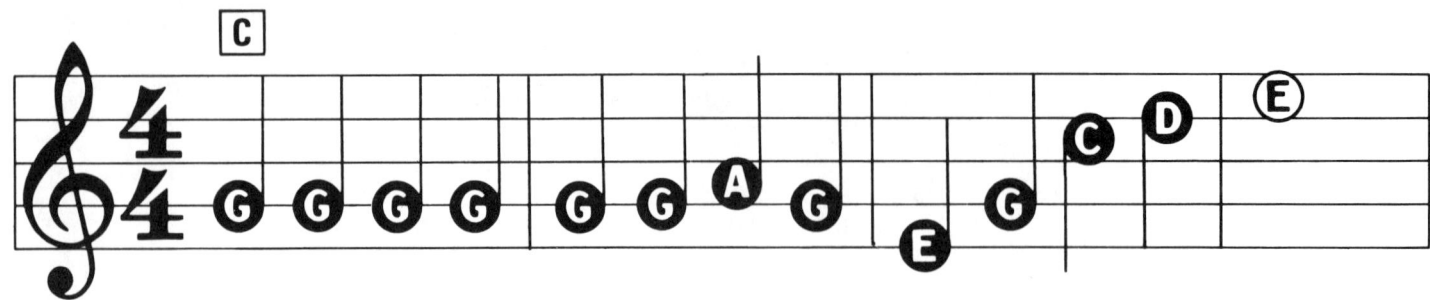

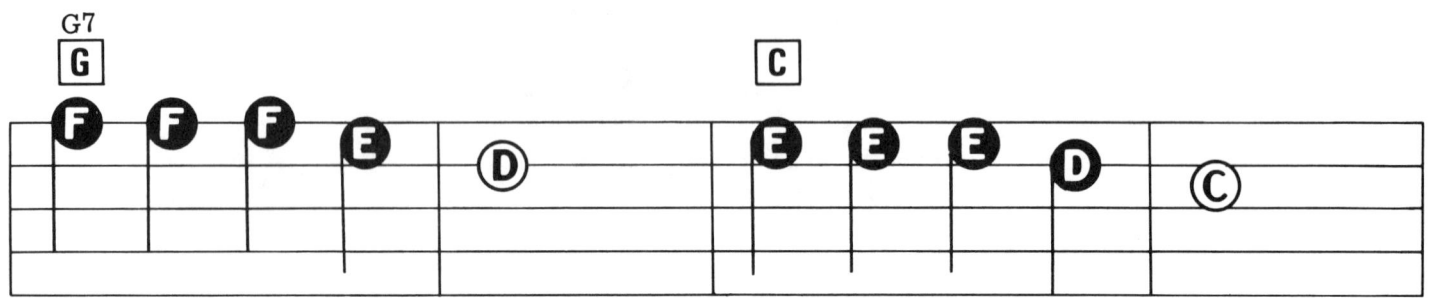

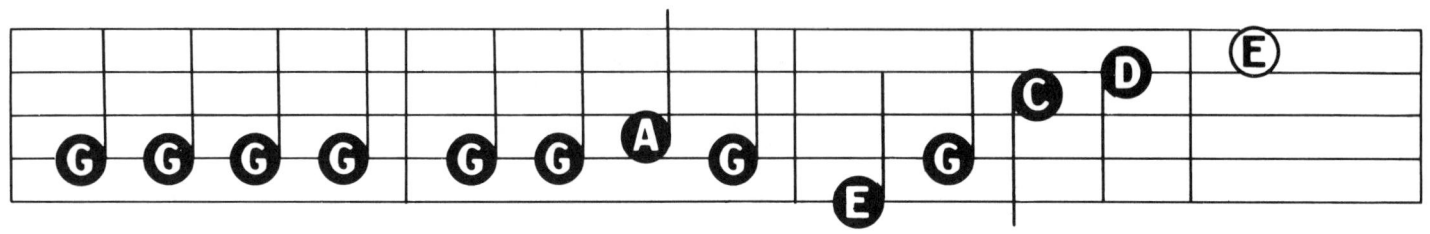

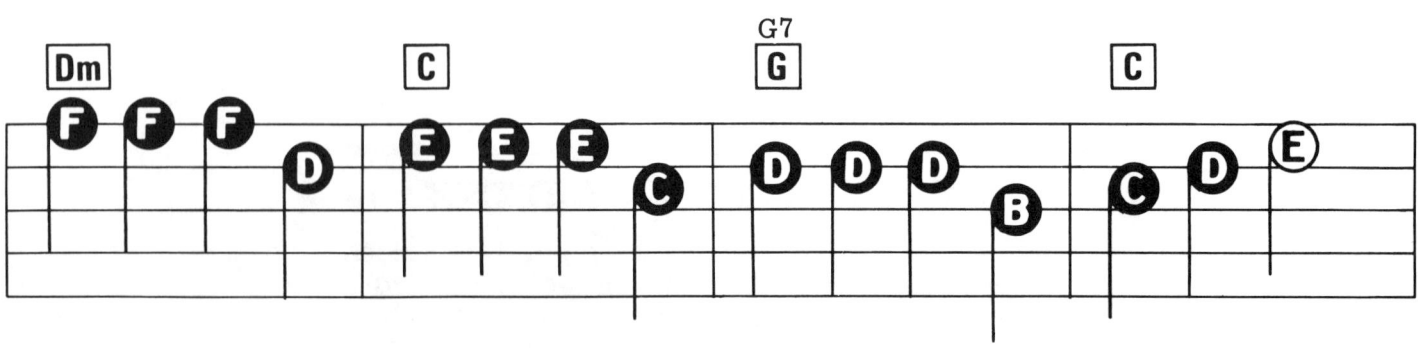

This arr. © Copyright 1976 by HAL LEONARD PUBLISHING CORPORATION, Winona, MN 55987
Made in U.S.A.   International Copyright Secured   All Rights Reserved

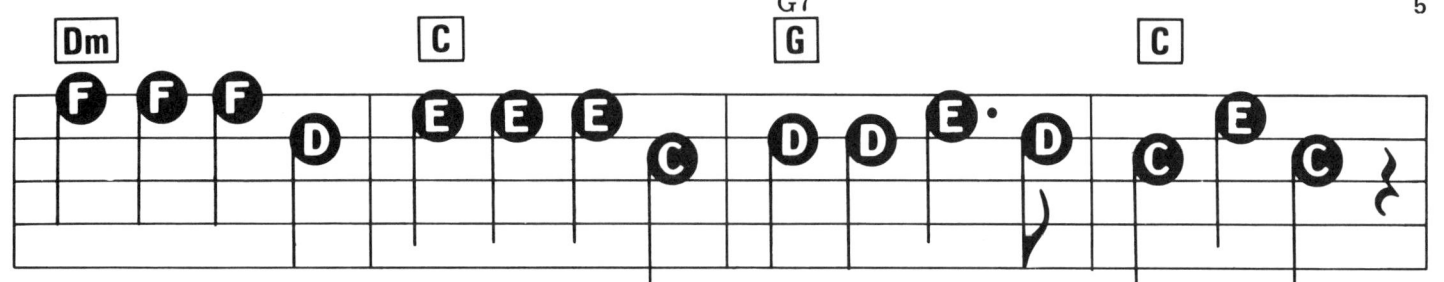
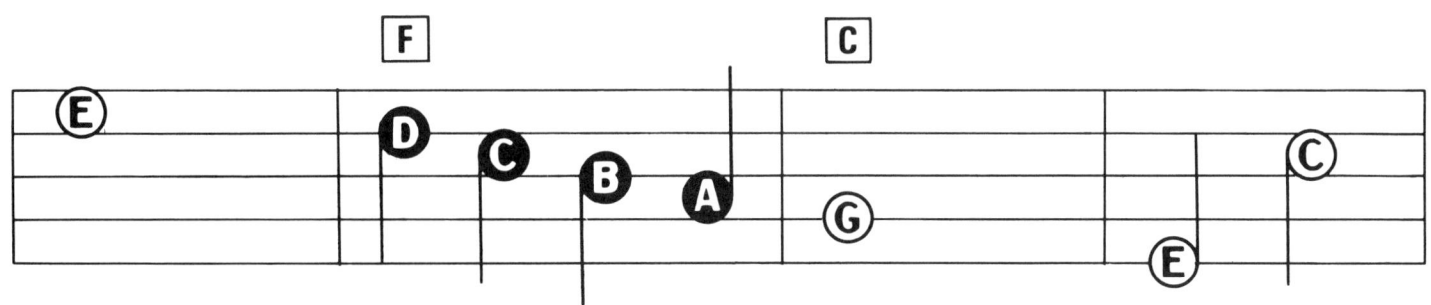
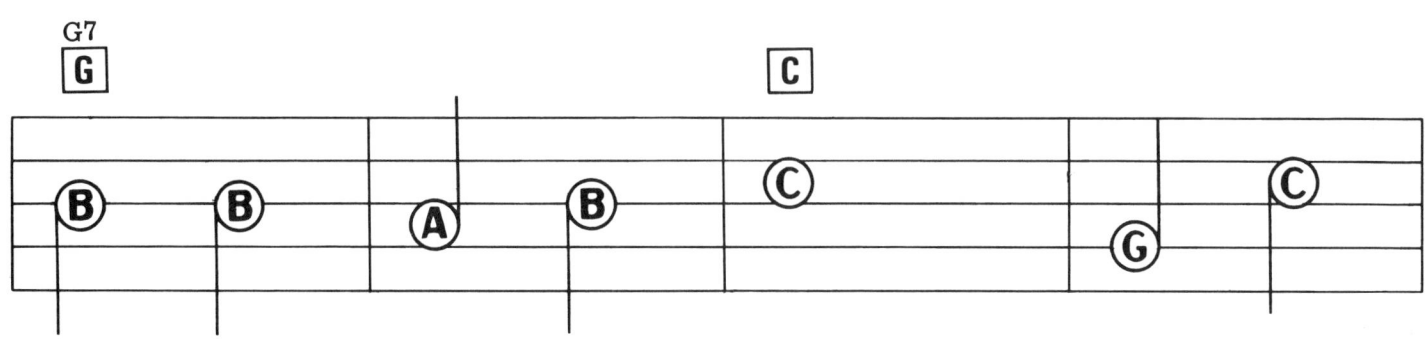
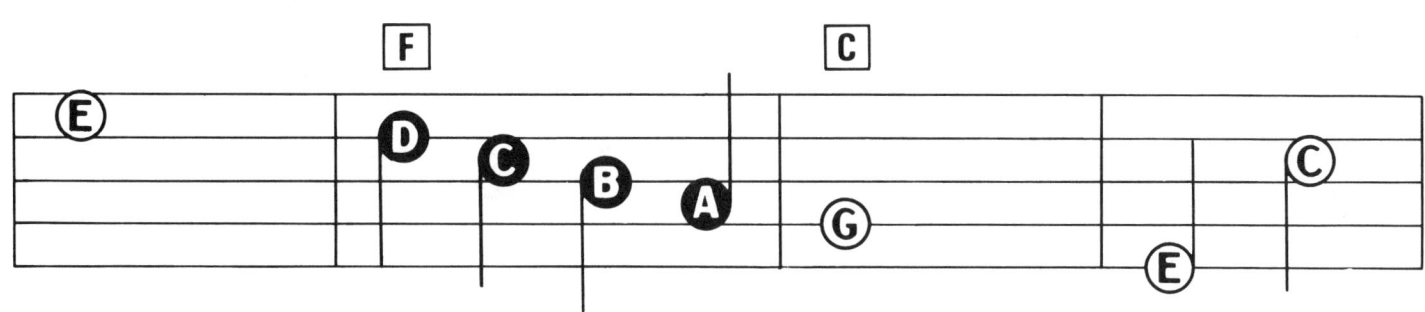
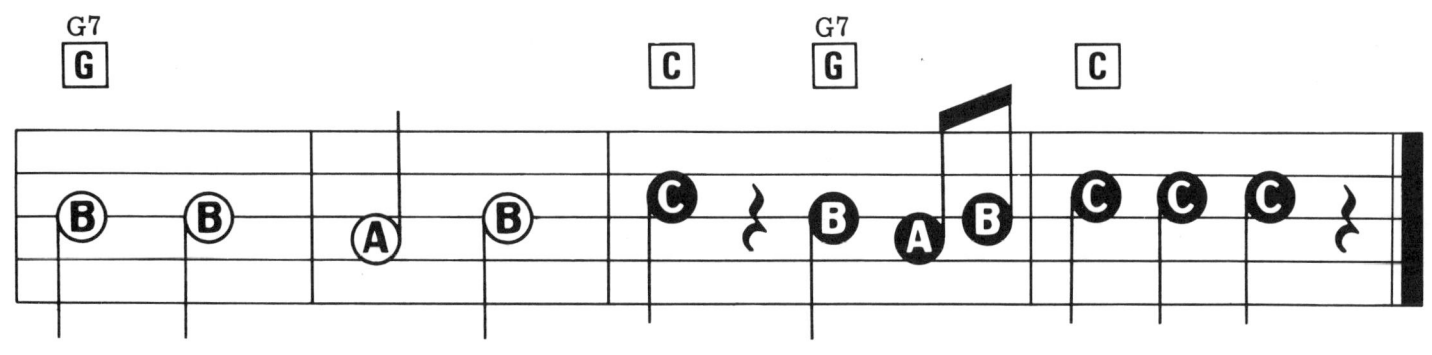

Can Can Polka

Registration 5

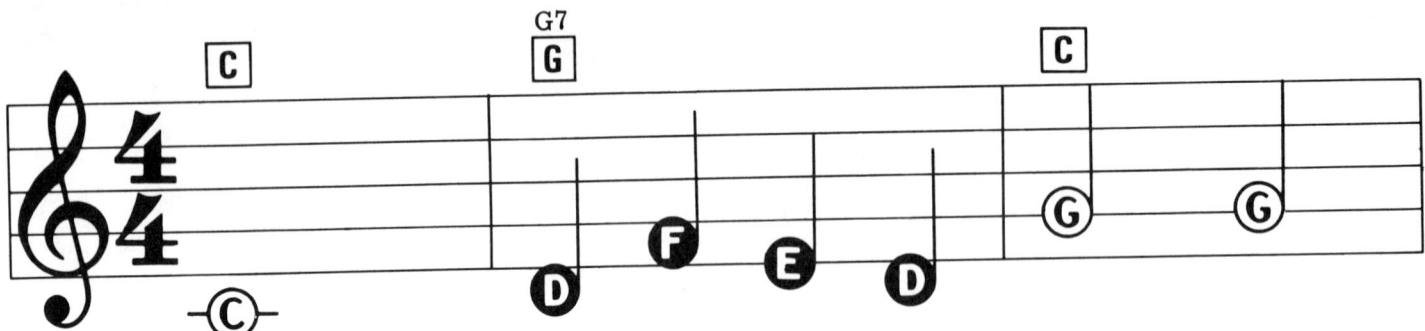
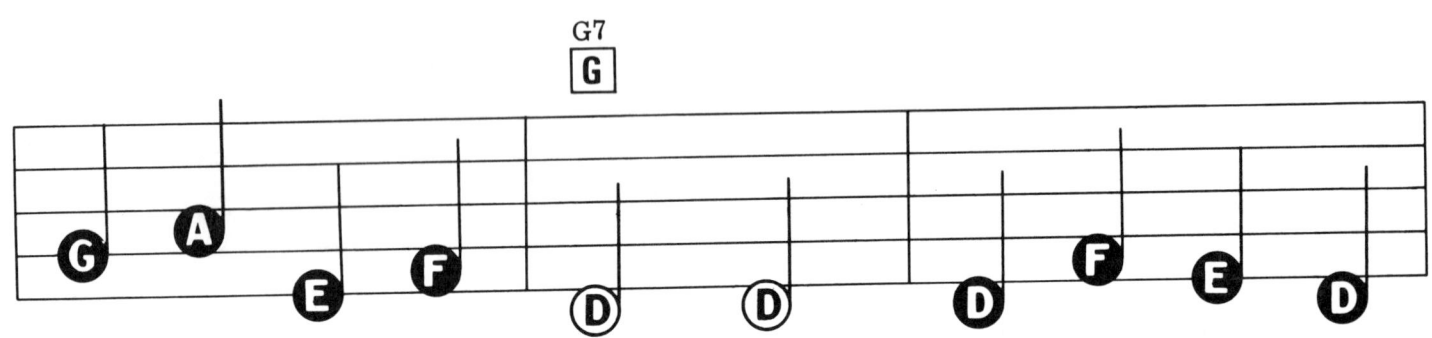
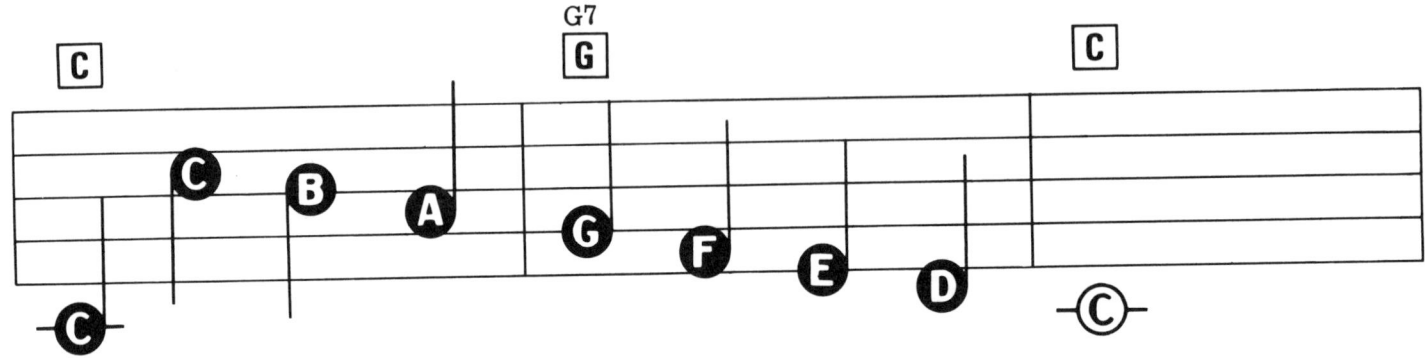
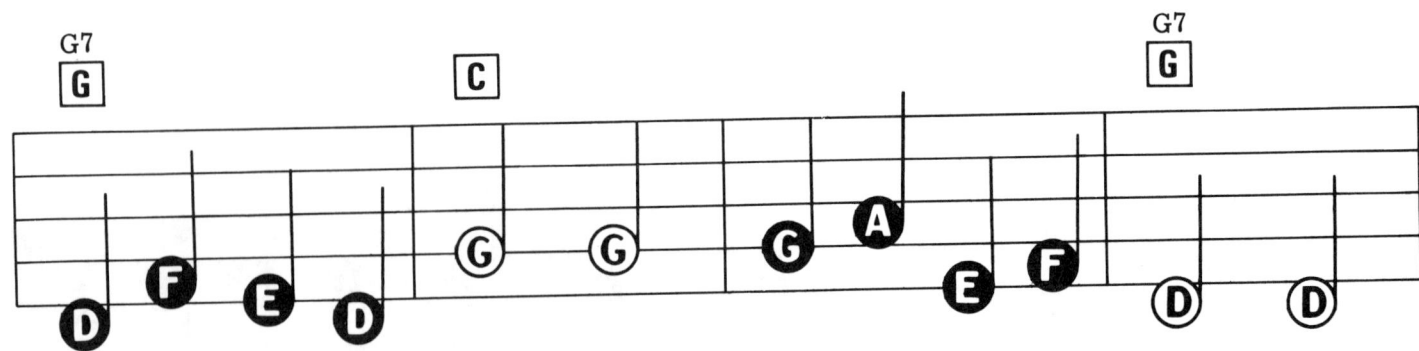

This arr. © Copyright 1976 by HAL LEONARD PUBLISHING CORPORATION, Winona, MN 55987
Made in U.S.A.   International Copyright Secured   All Rights Reserved

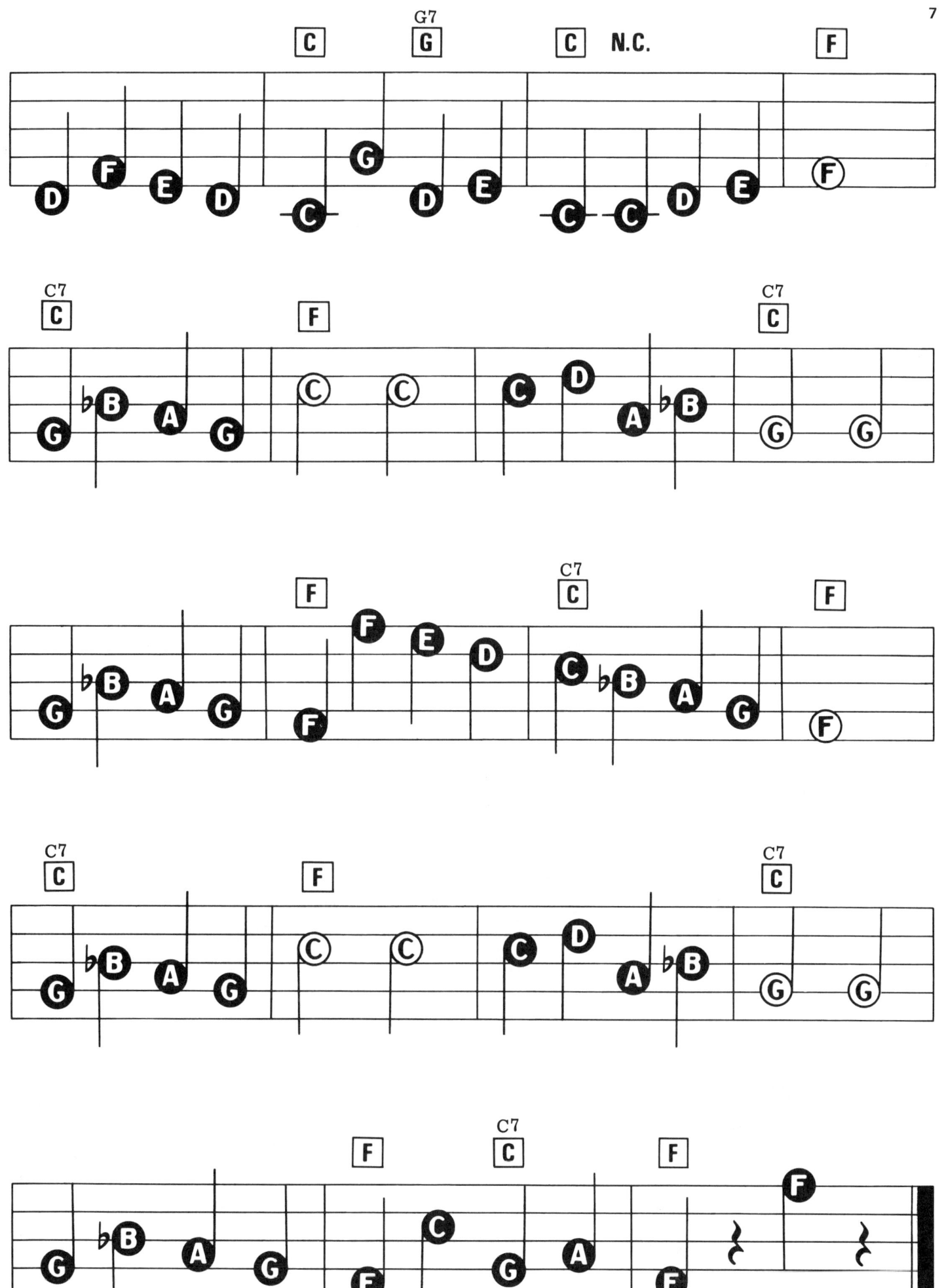

Clarinet Polka

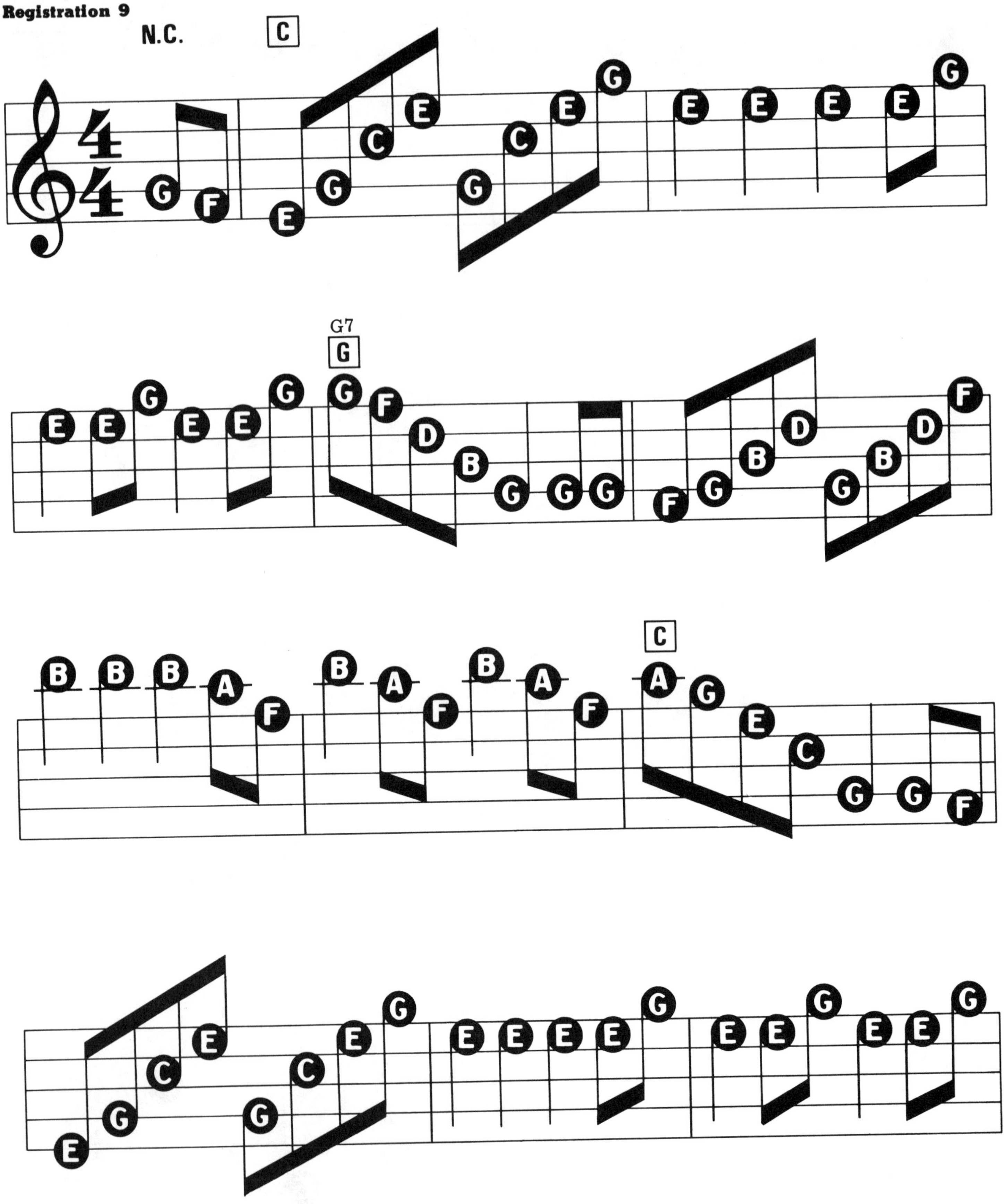

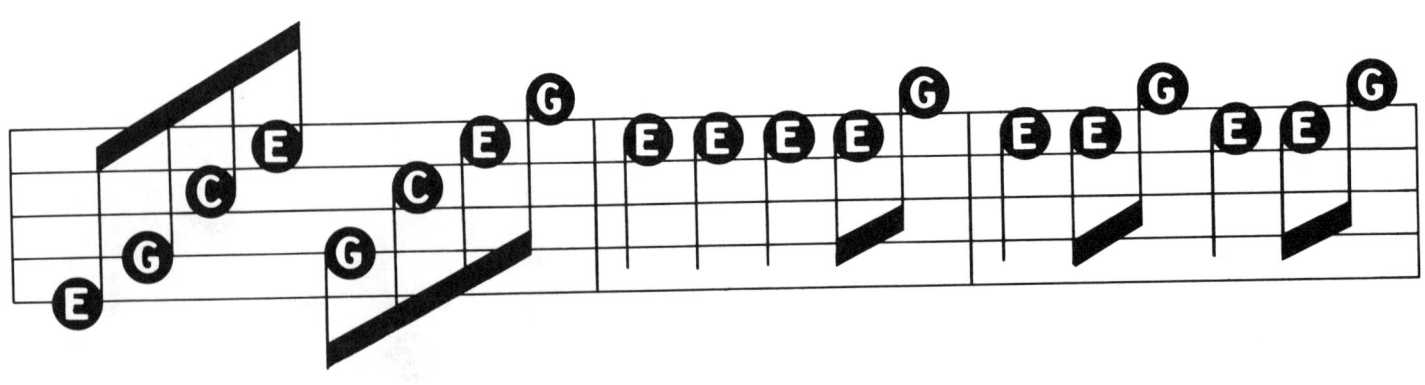

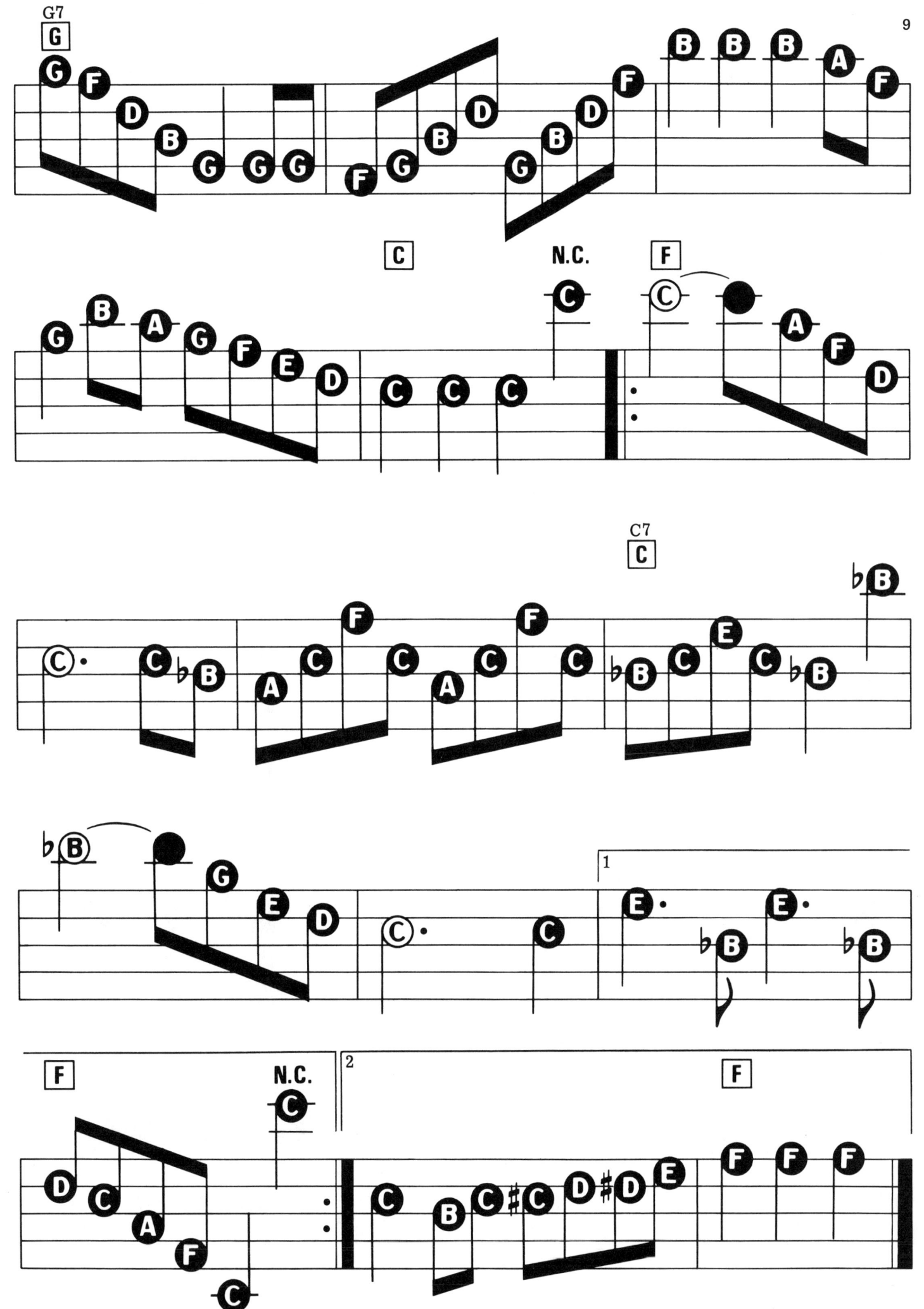

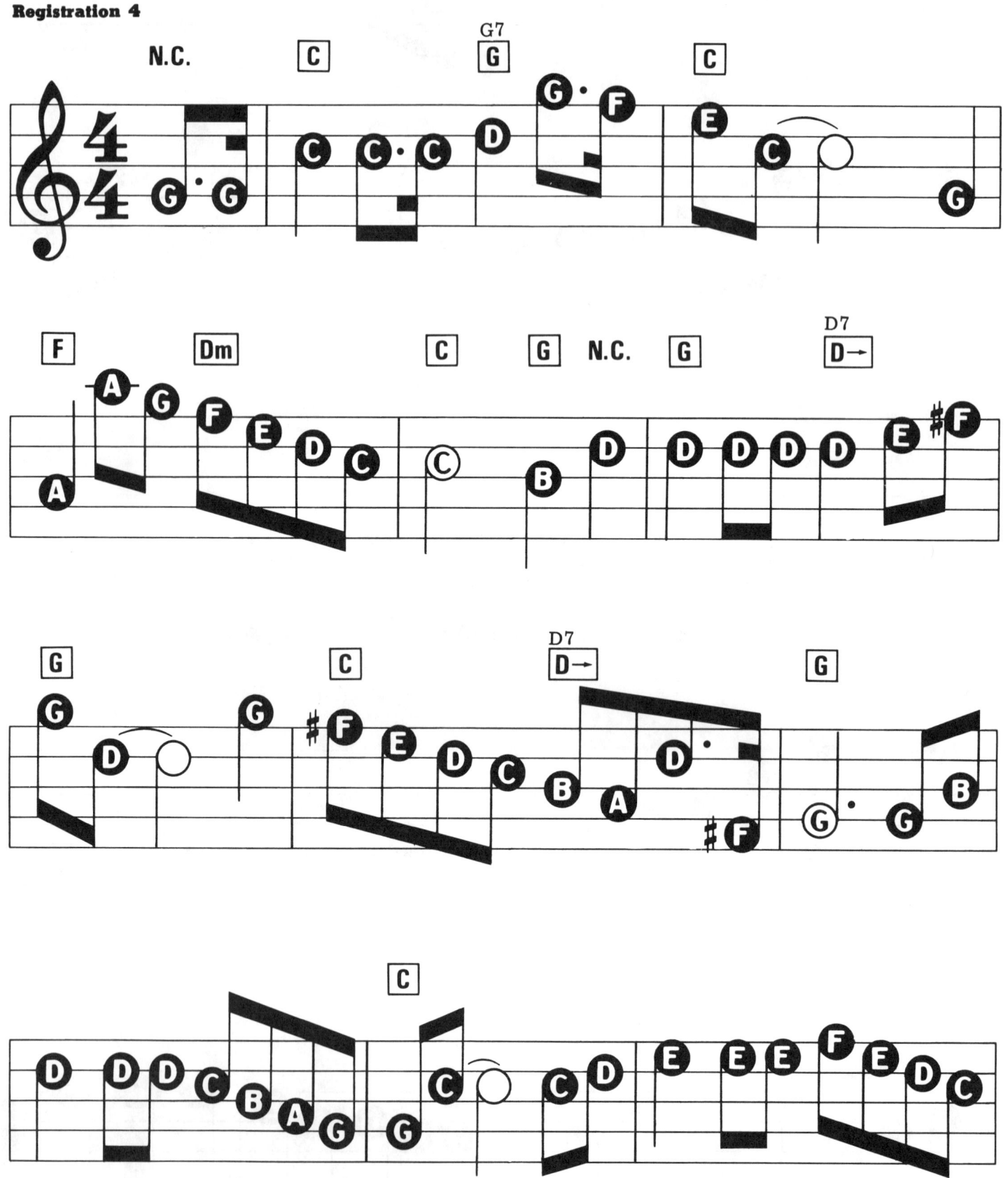

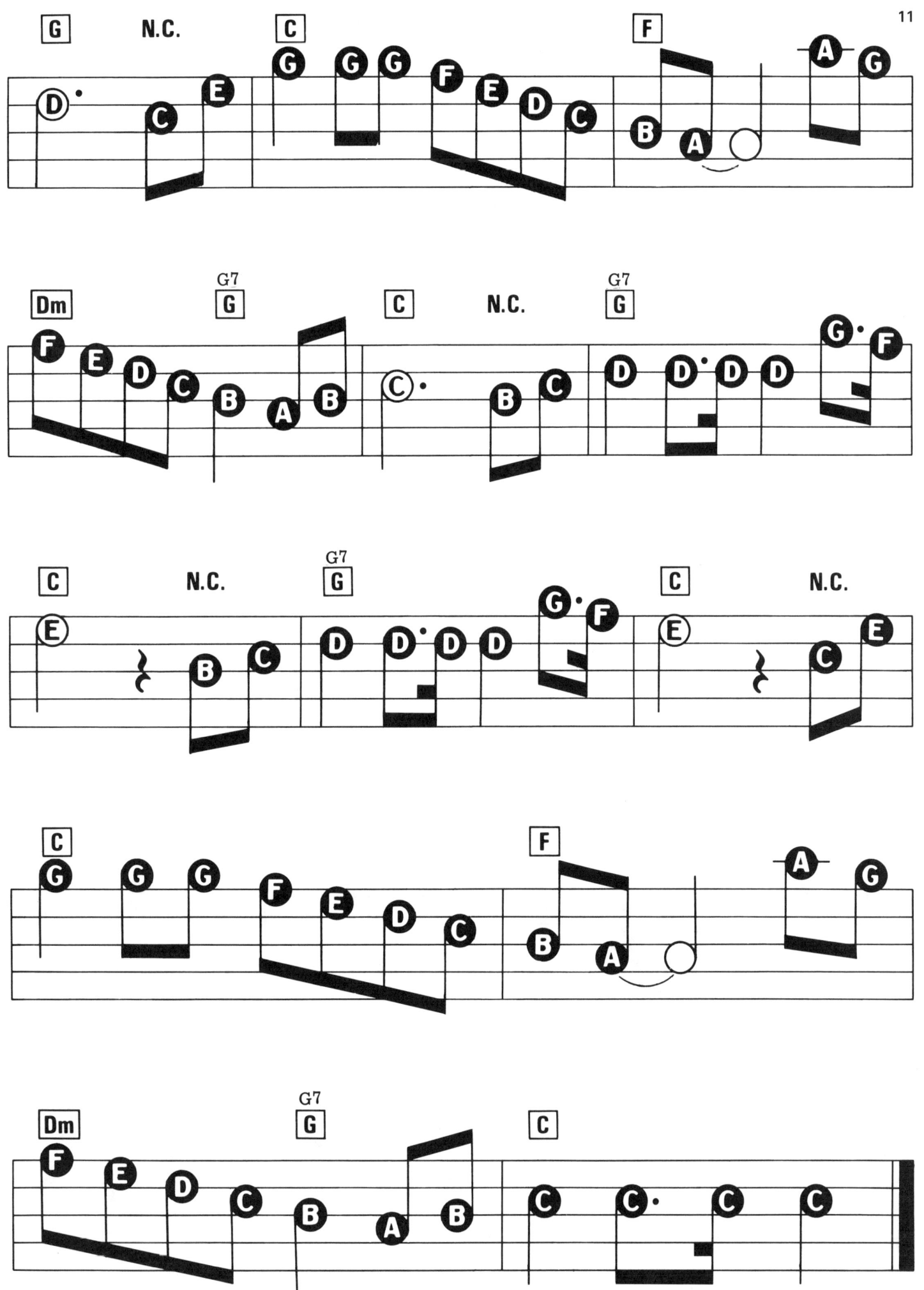

Friendly Fellows Polka

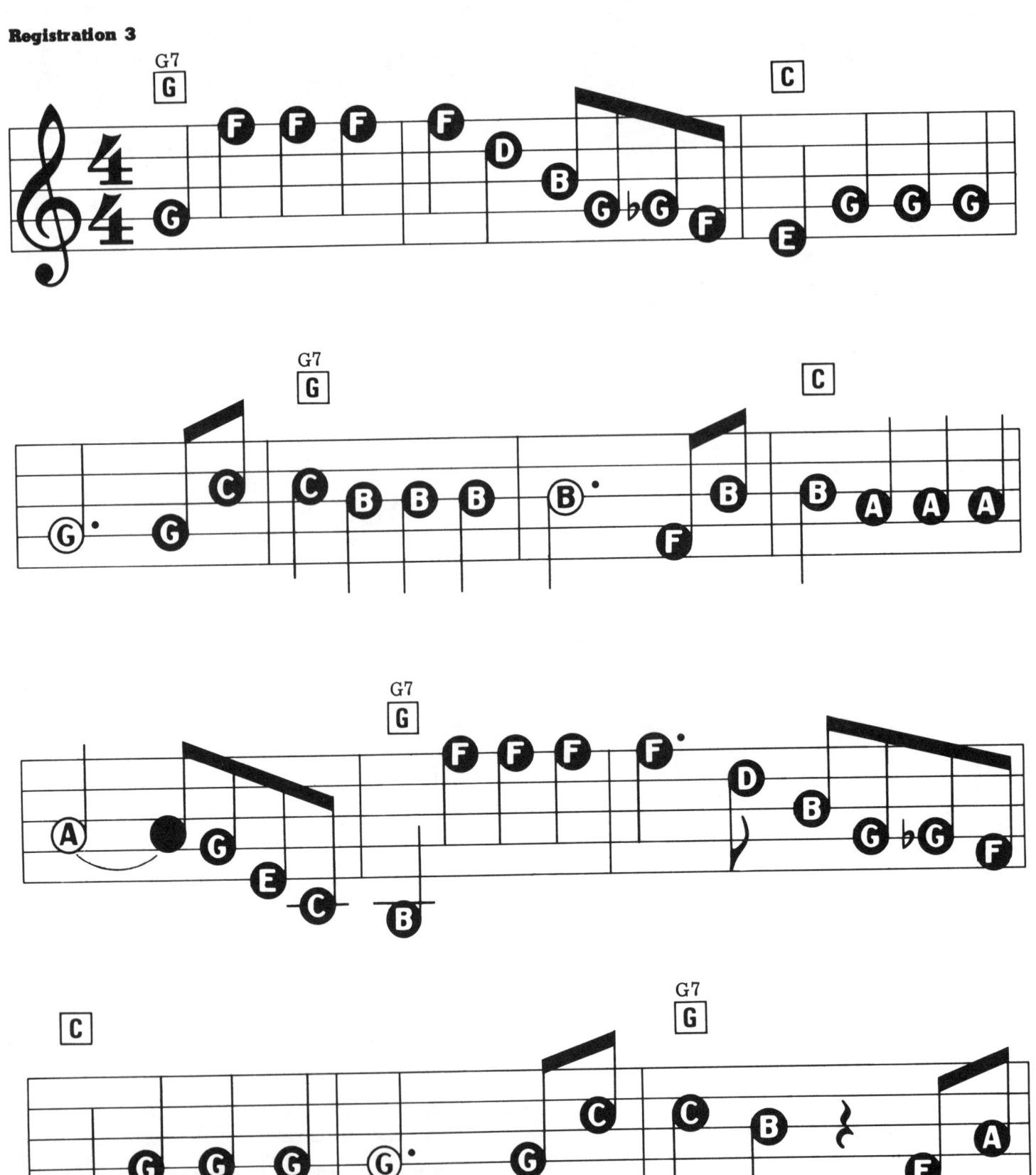

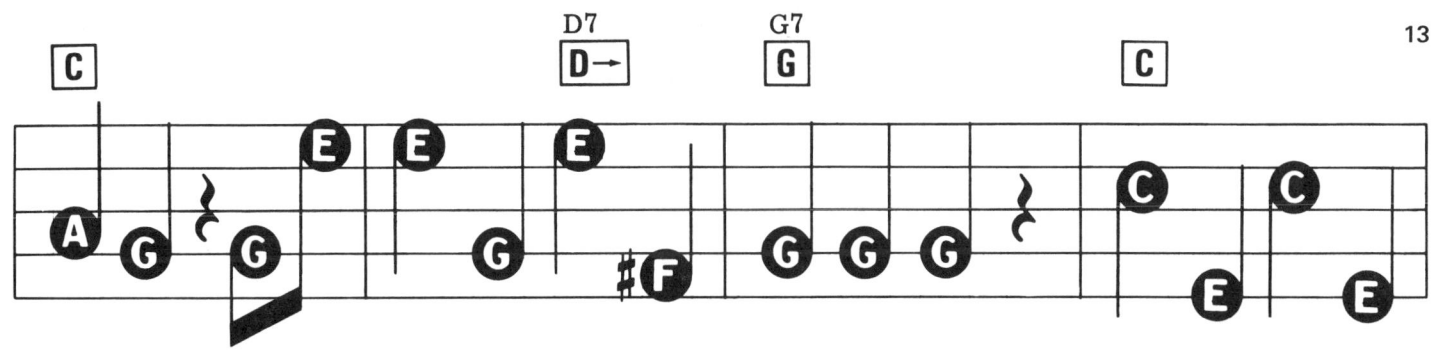
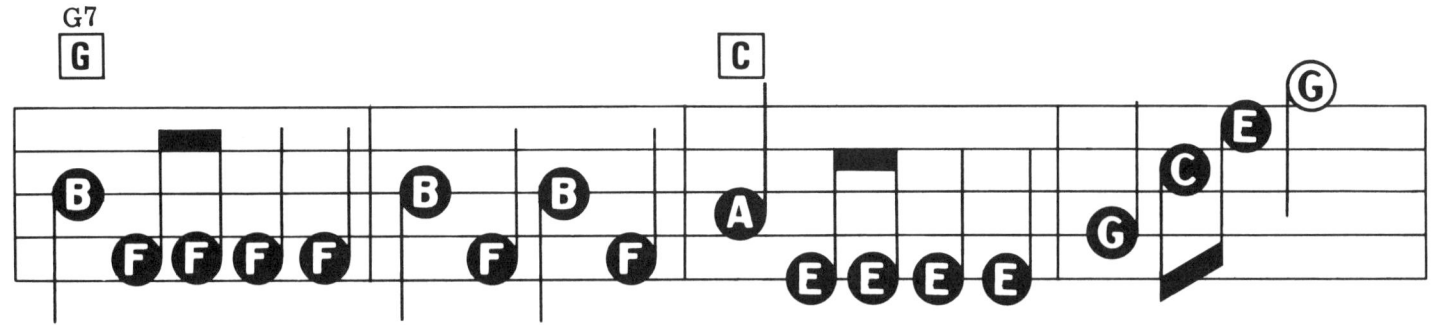
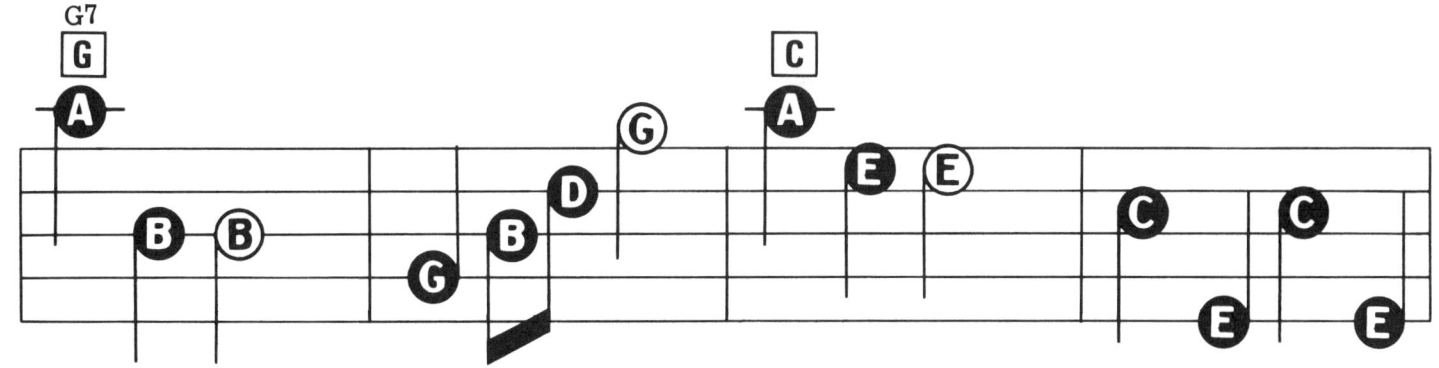
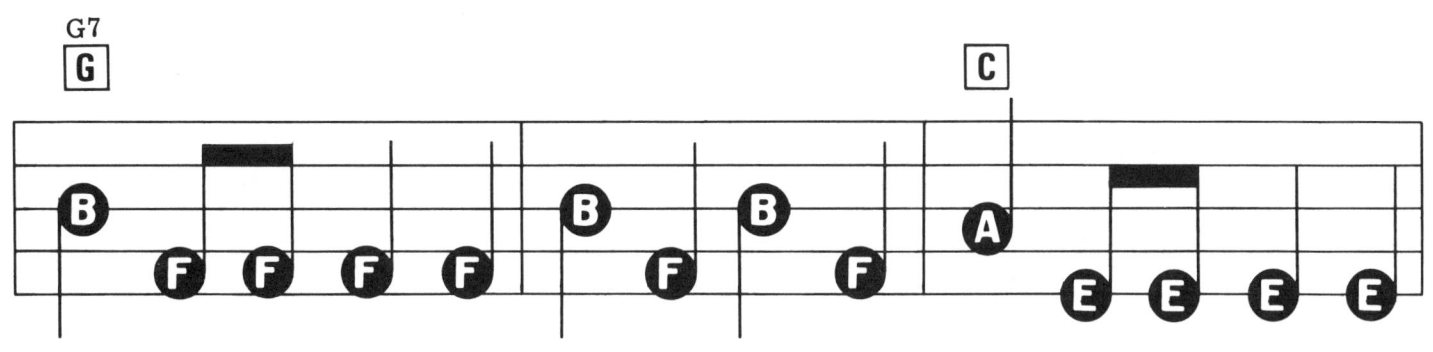
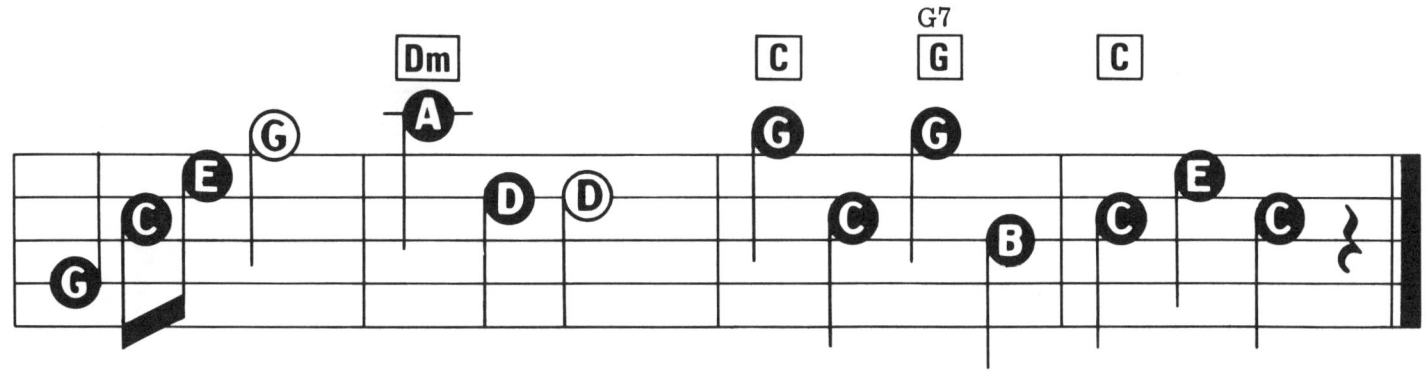

Helena Polka

Registration 9

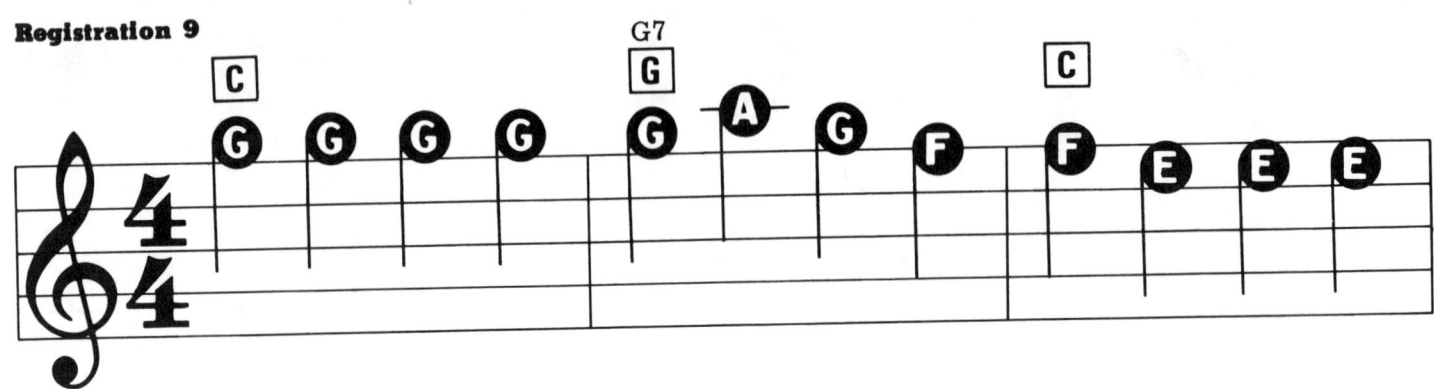
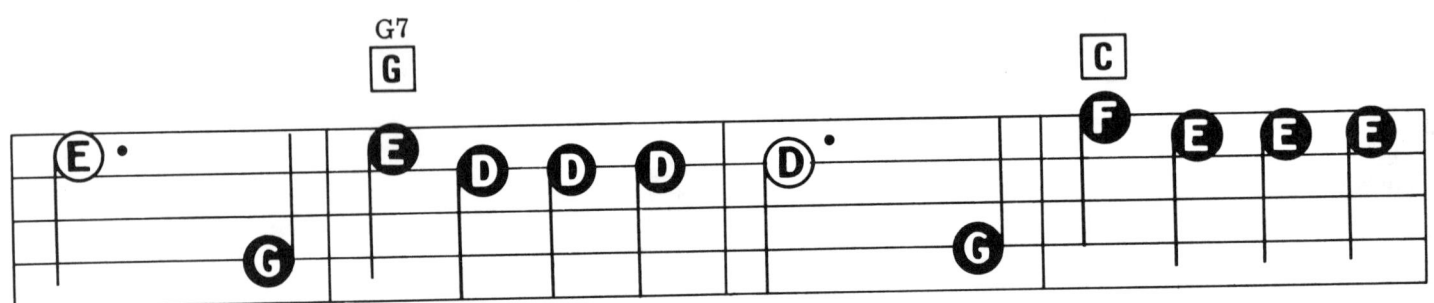
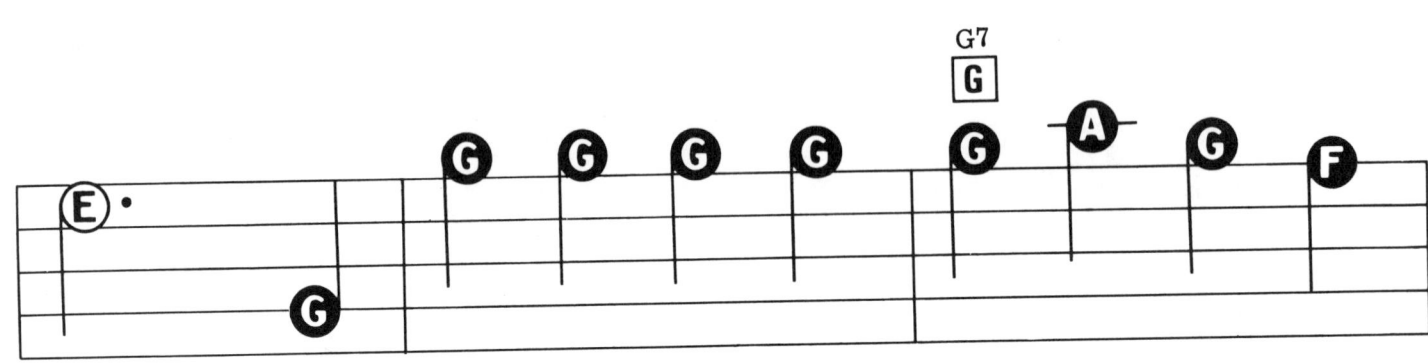
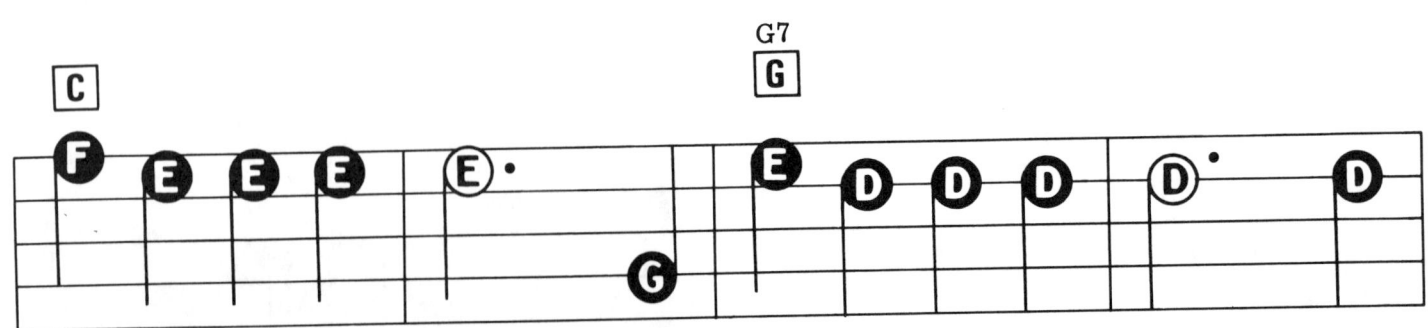

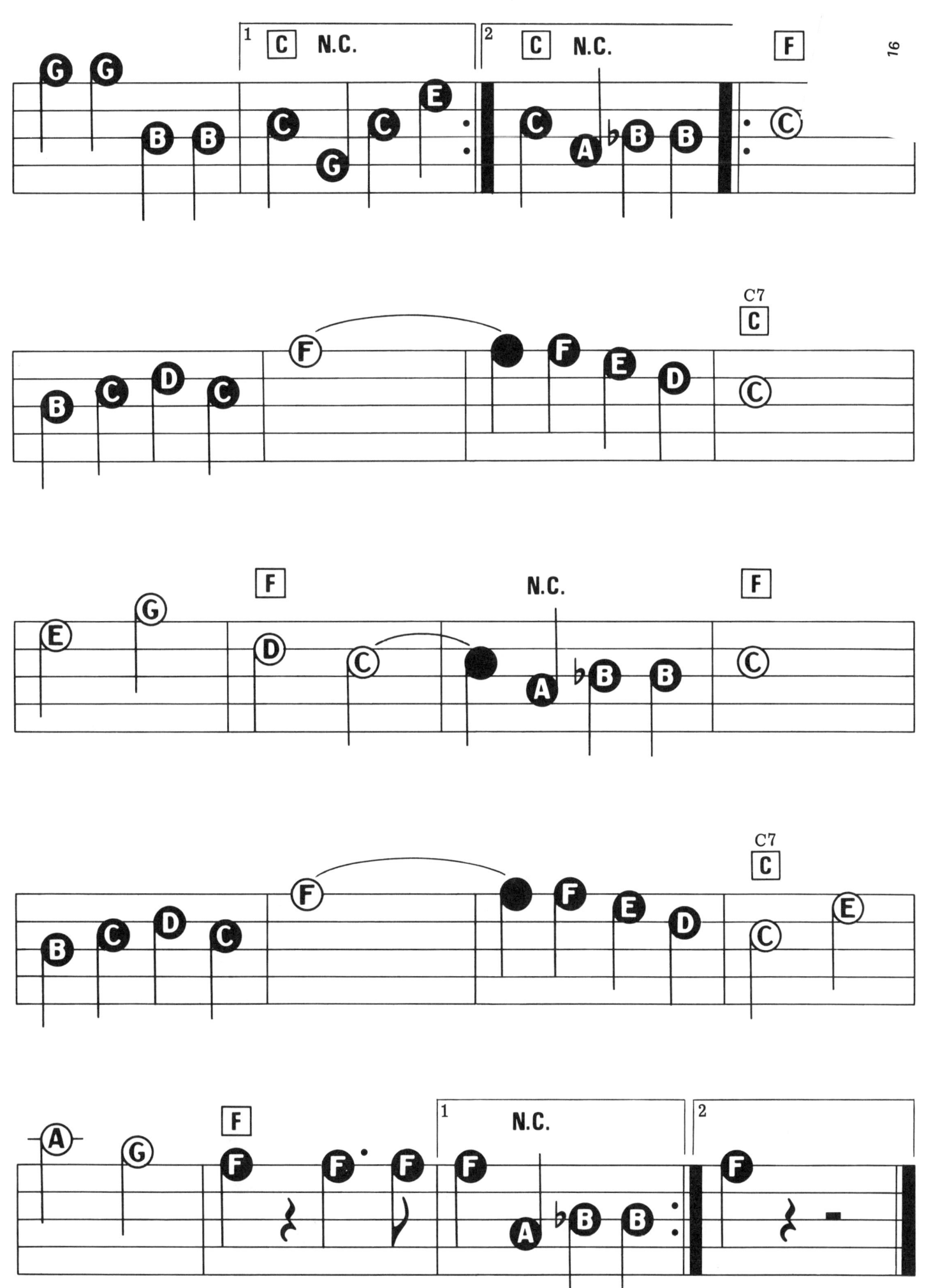

High School Cadets

Registration 2

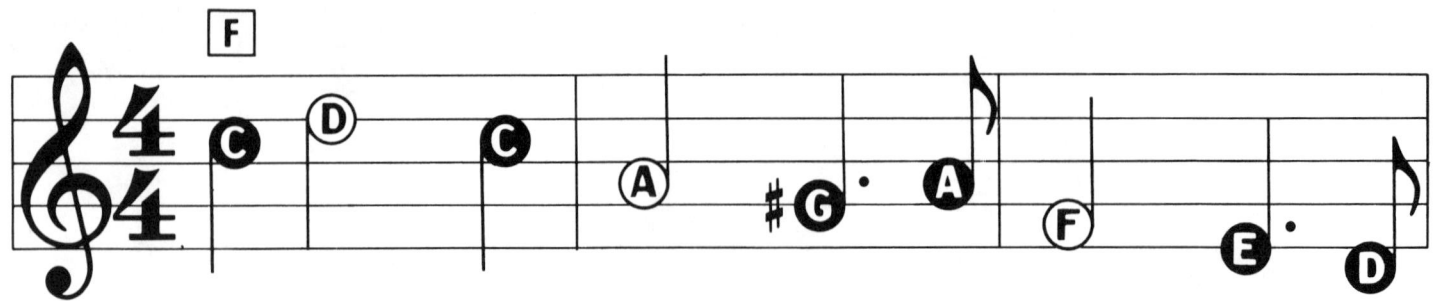
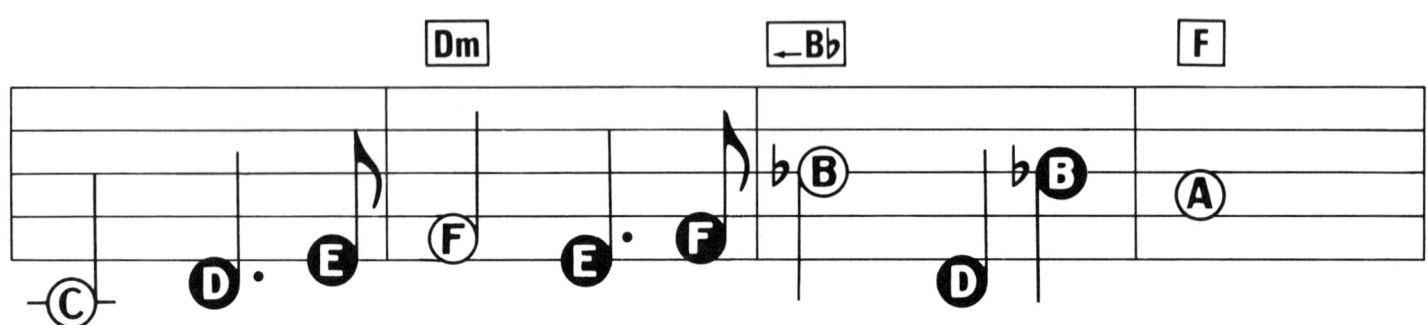
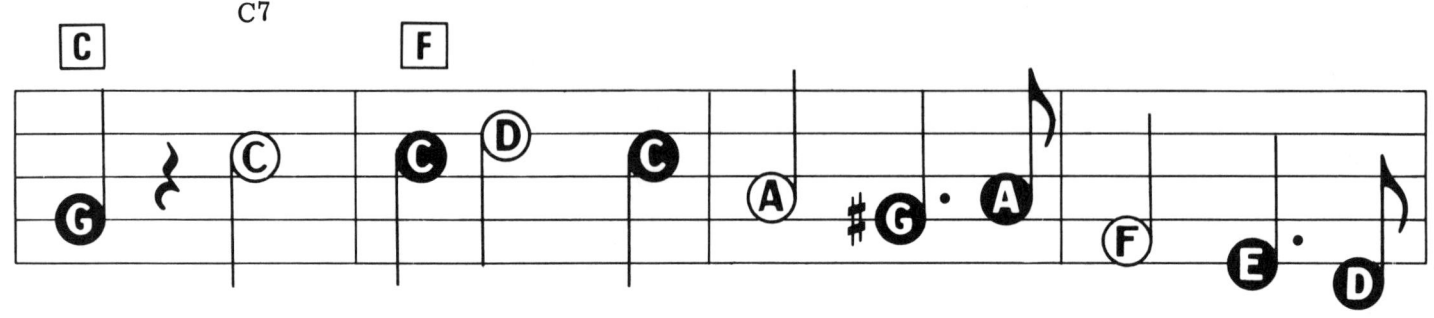
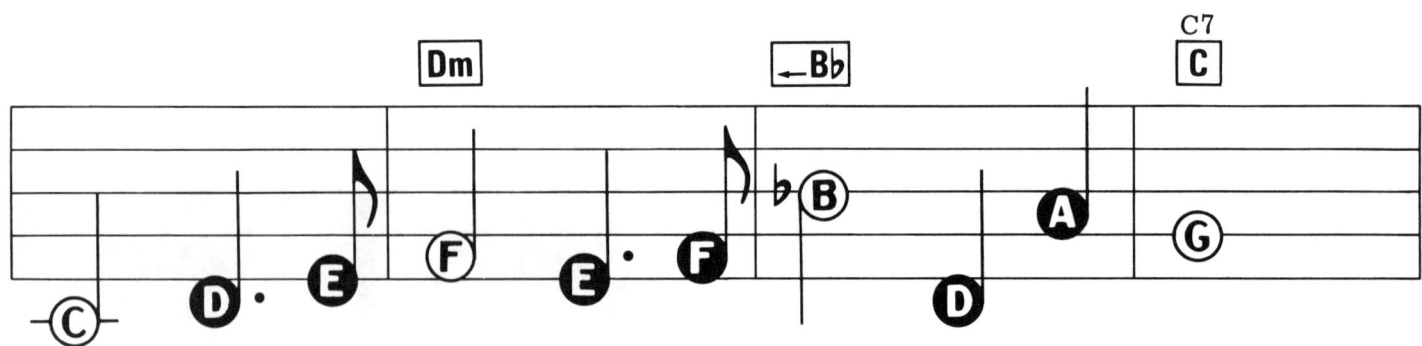

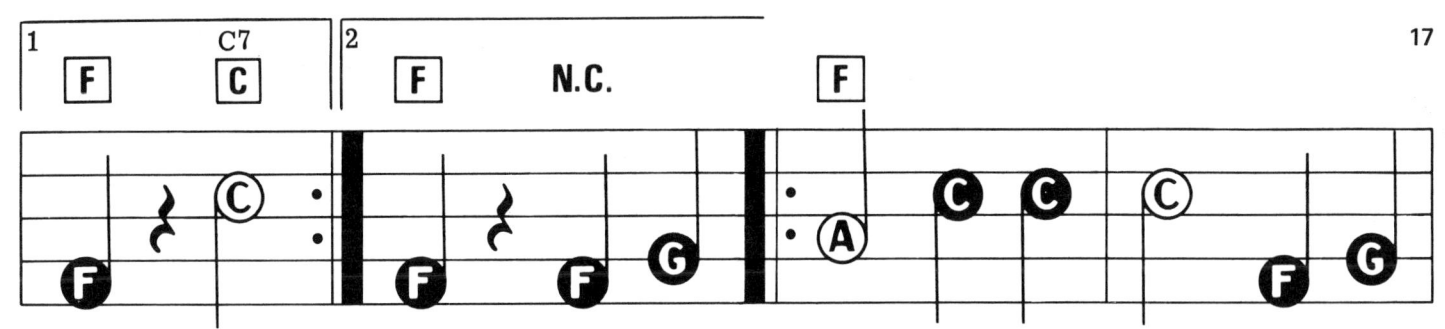
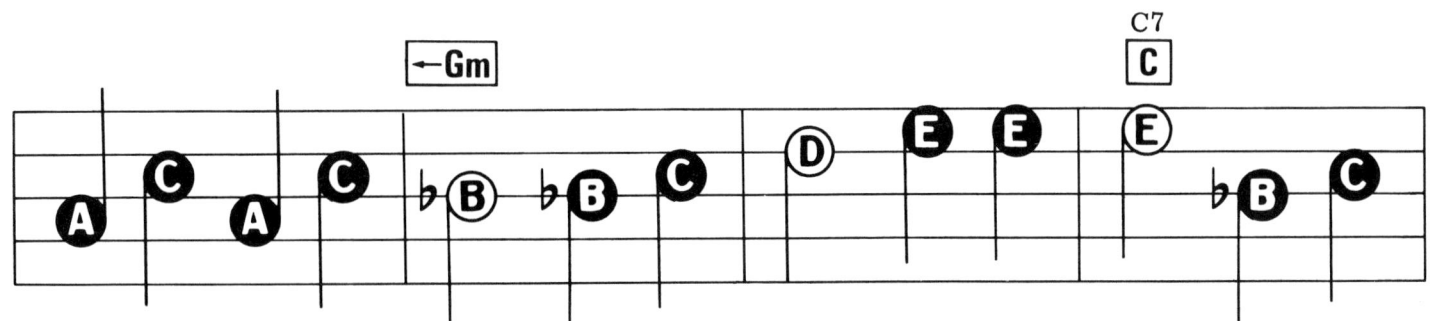
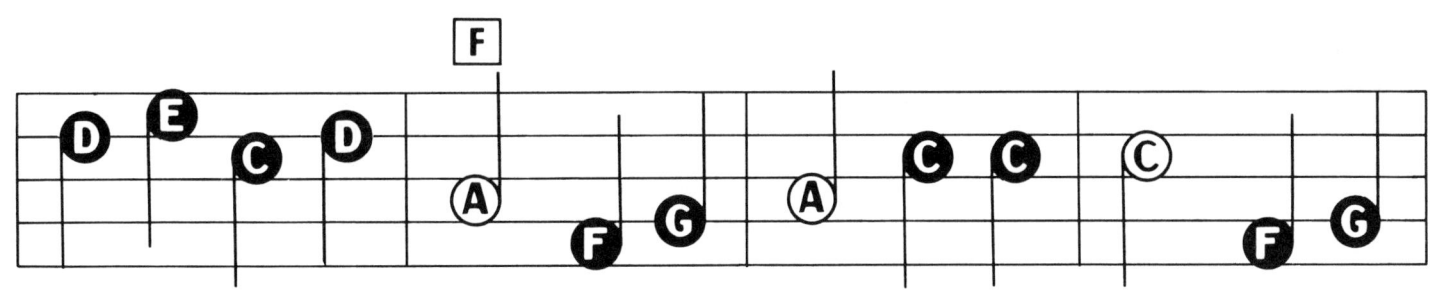
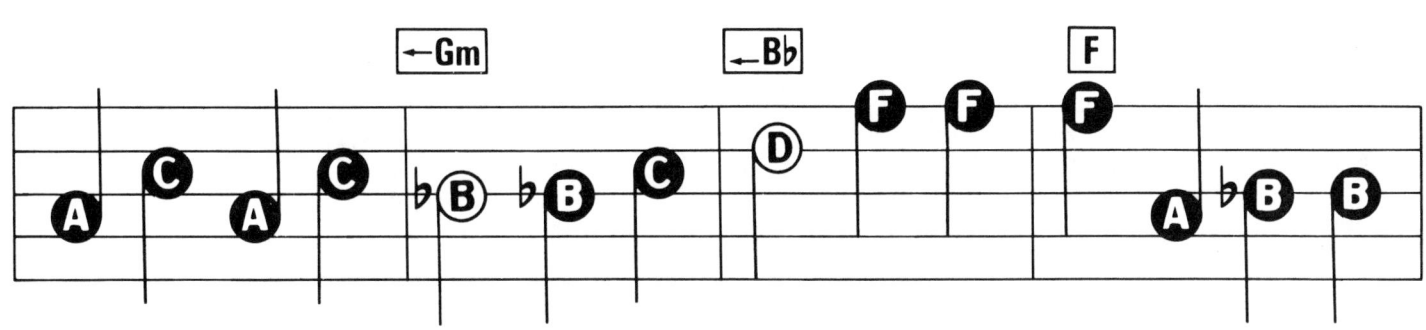
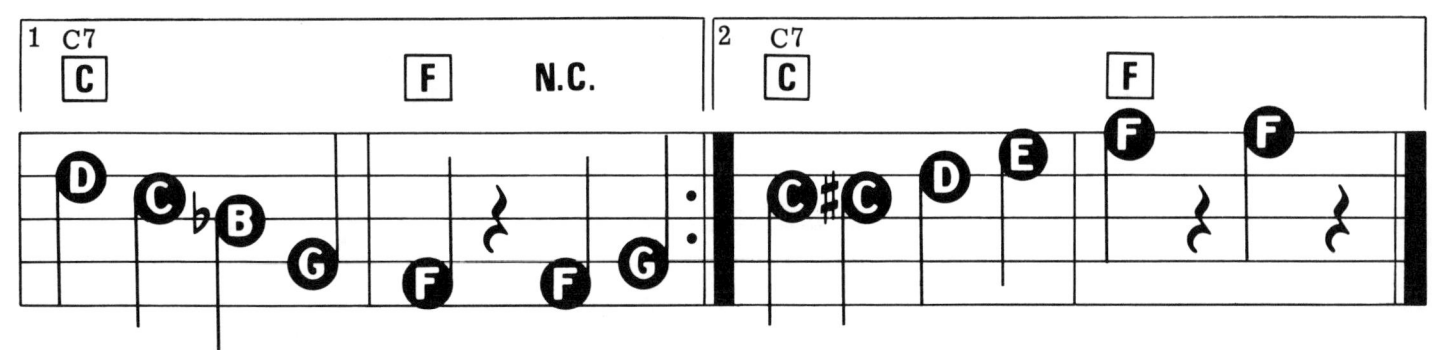

Julida Polka

Registration 4

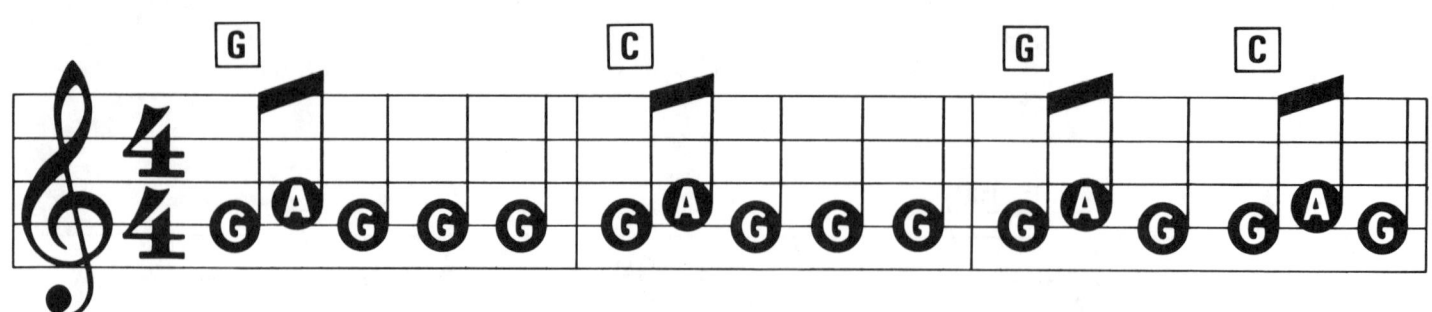
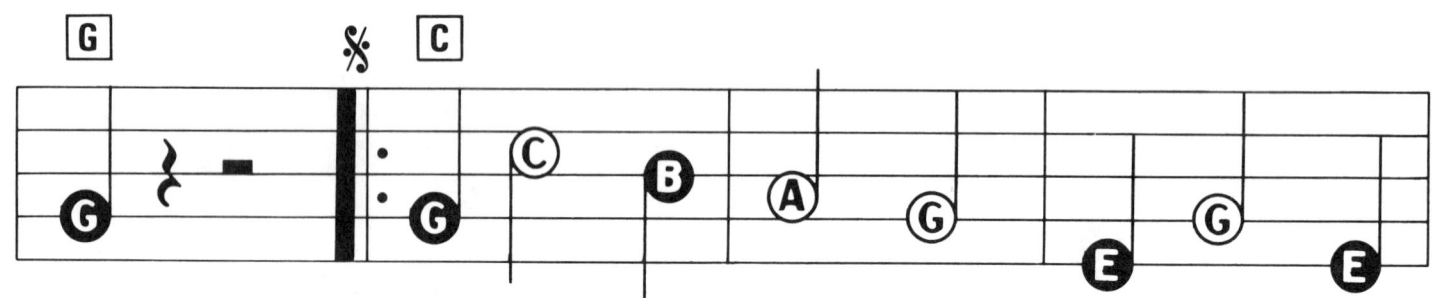
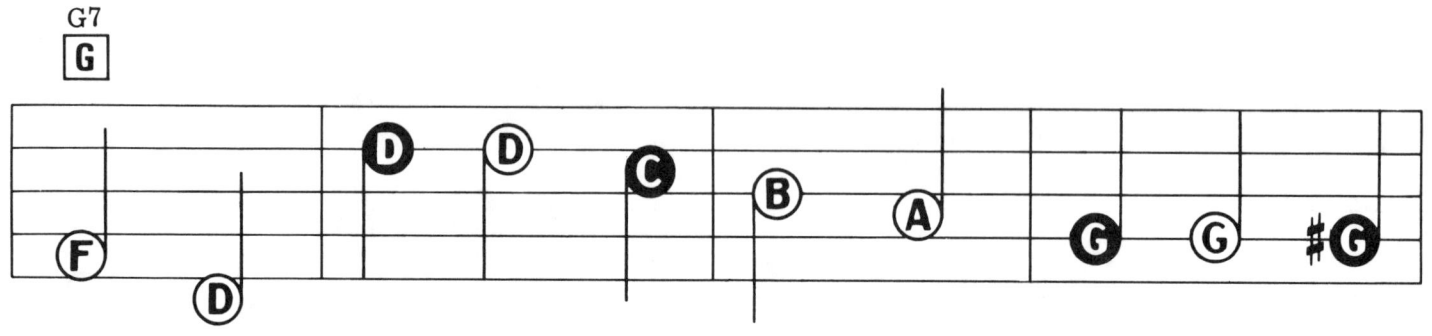
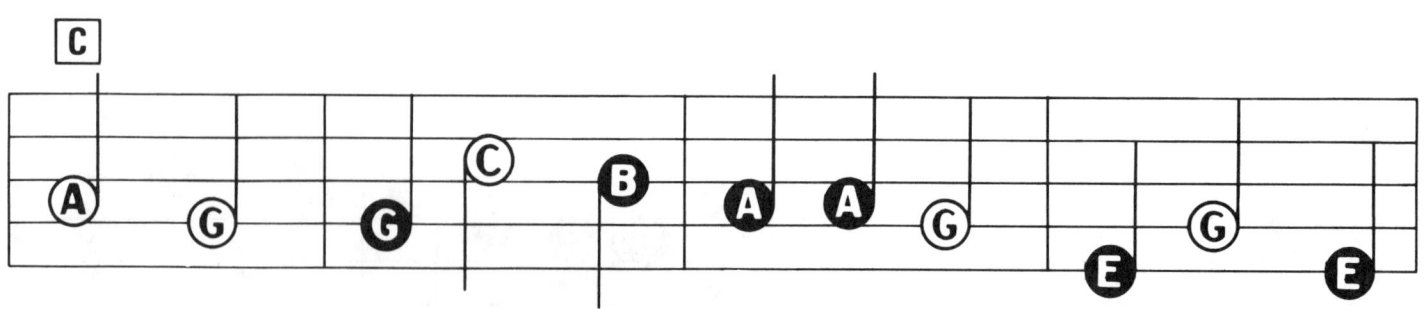

This arr. © Copyright 1976 by HAL LEONARD PUBLISHING CORPORATION, Winona, MN 55987
Made in U.S.A.   International Copyright Secured   All Rights Reserved

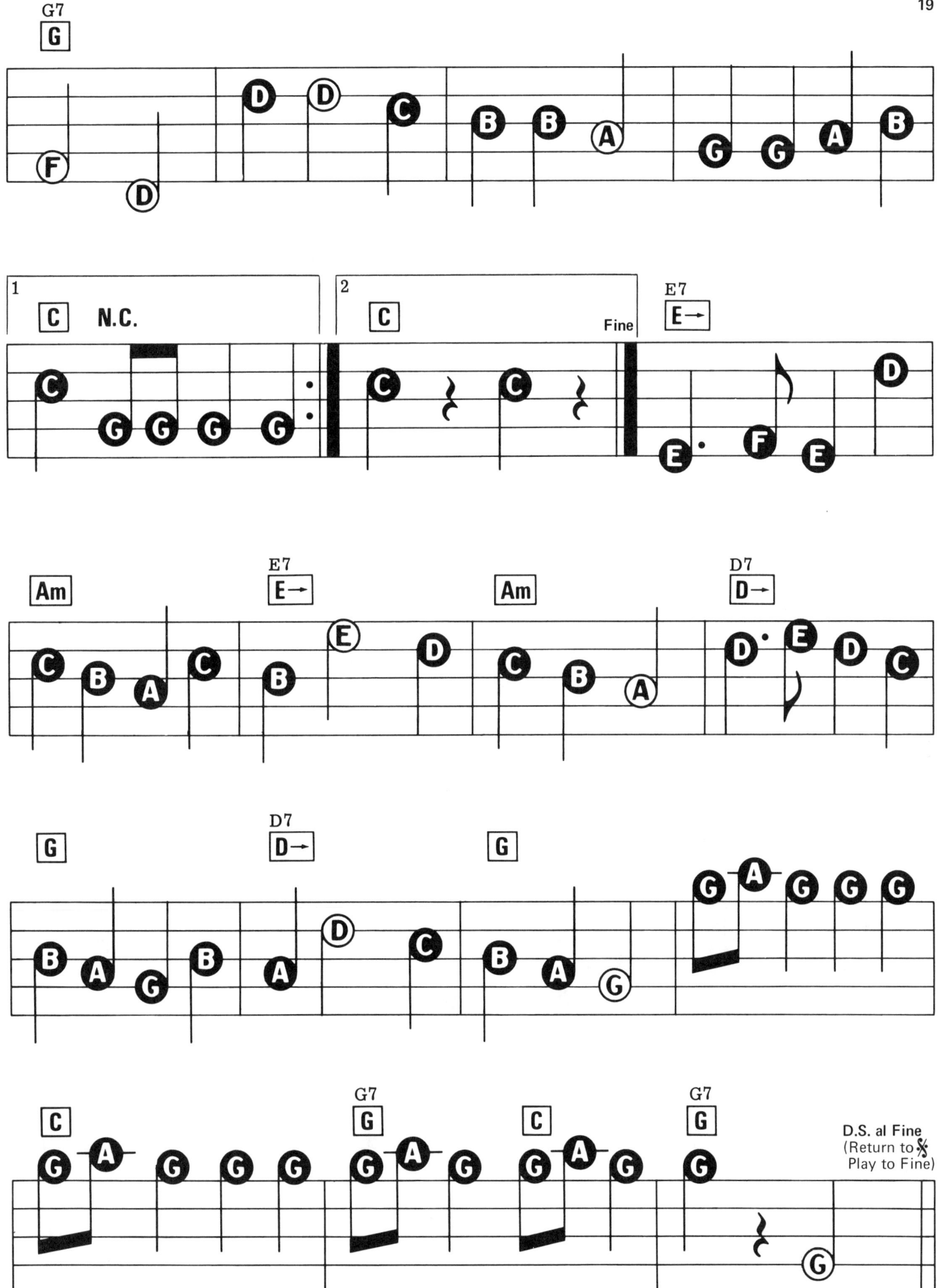

King Cotton March

Registration 5

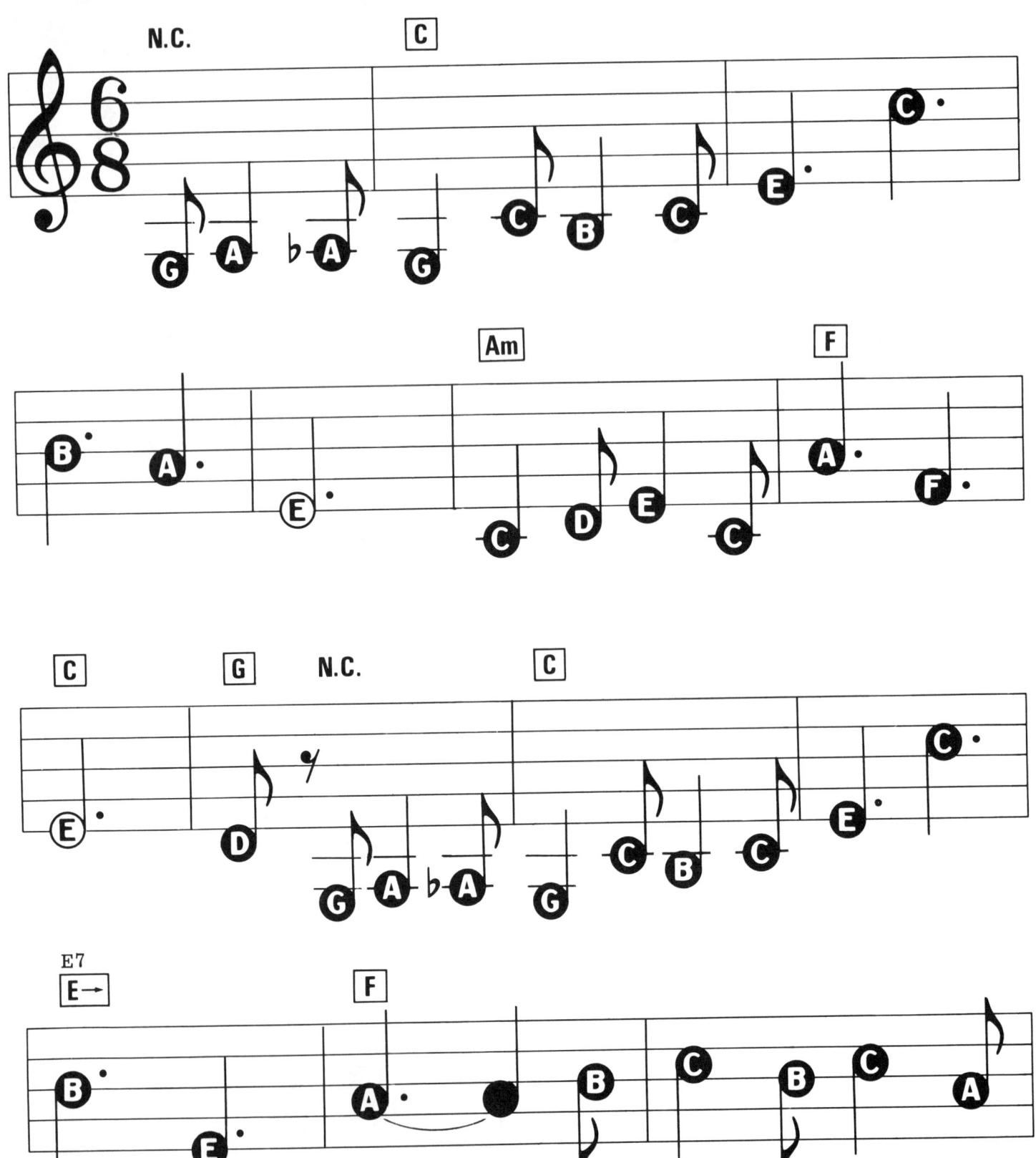

This arr. © Copyright 1976 by HAL LEONARD PUBLISHING CORPORATION, Winona, MN 55987
Made in U.S.A.   International Copyright Secured   All Rights Reserved

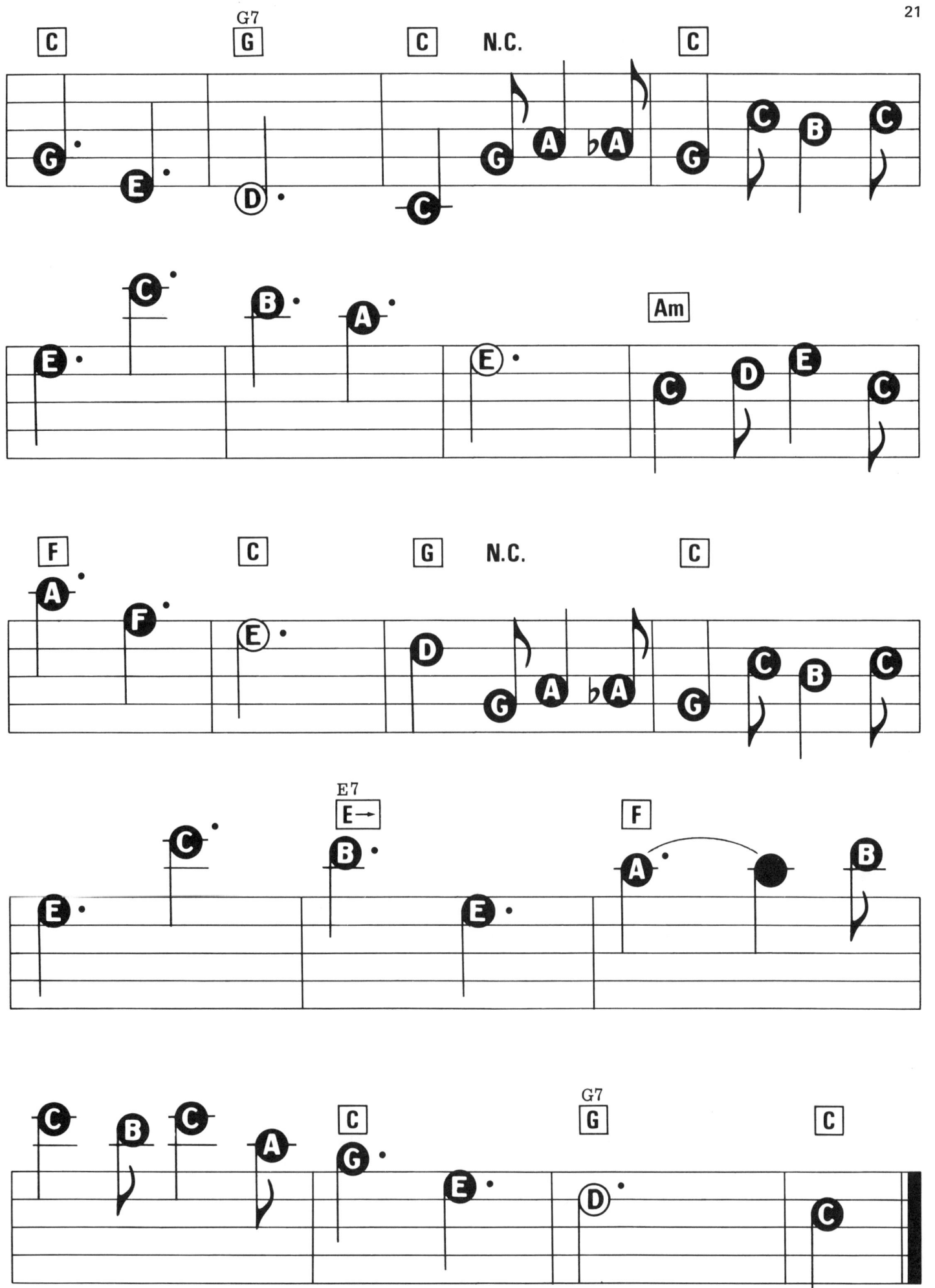

La-La-La Polka

Registration 8

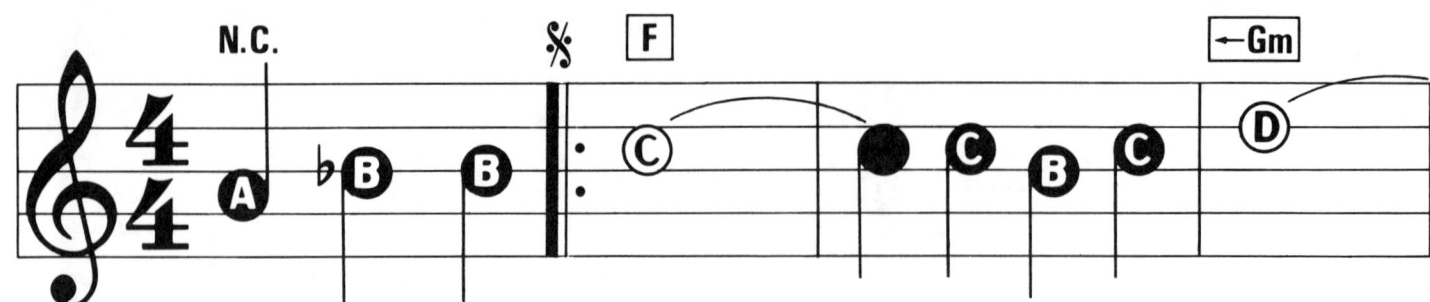
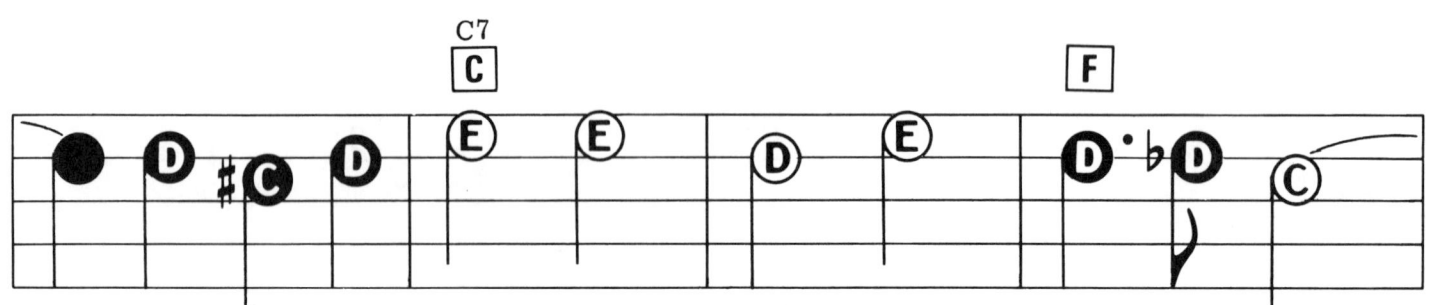
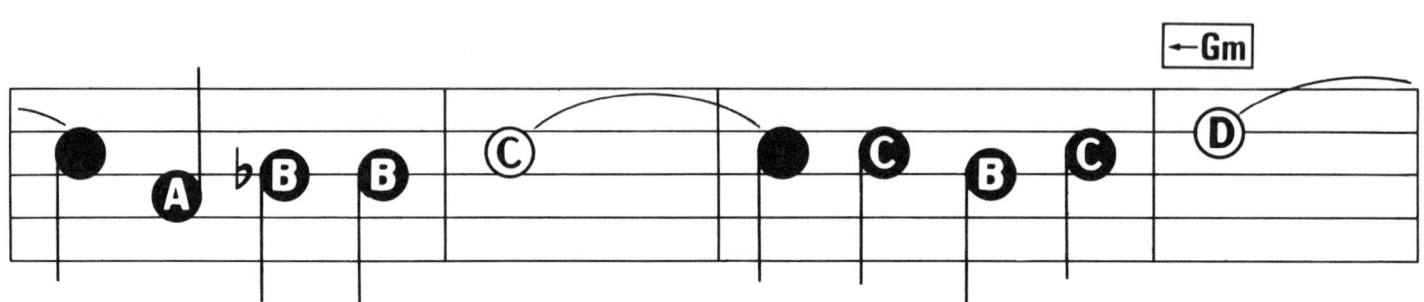
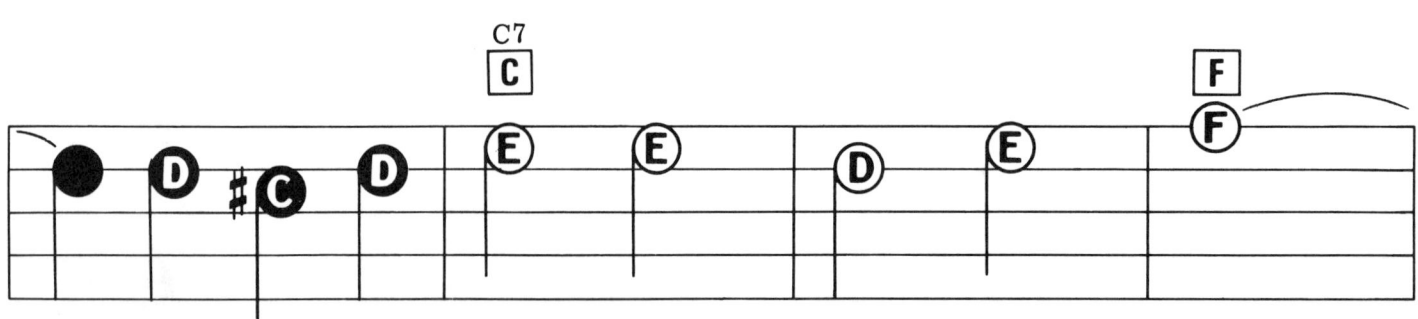

This arr. © Copyright 1976 by HAL LEONARD PUBLISHING CORPORATION, Winona, MN 55987
Made in U.S.A.   International Copyright Secured   All Rights Reserved

23

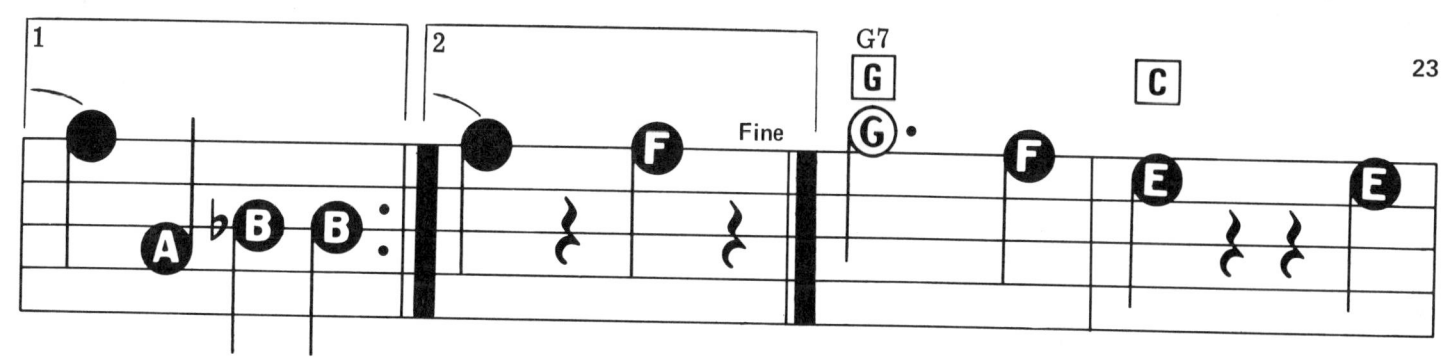
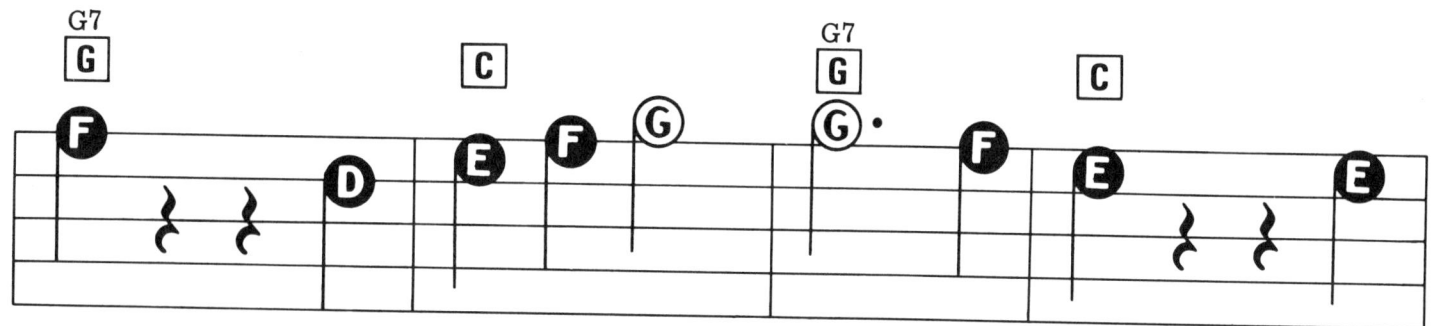
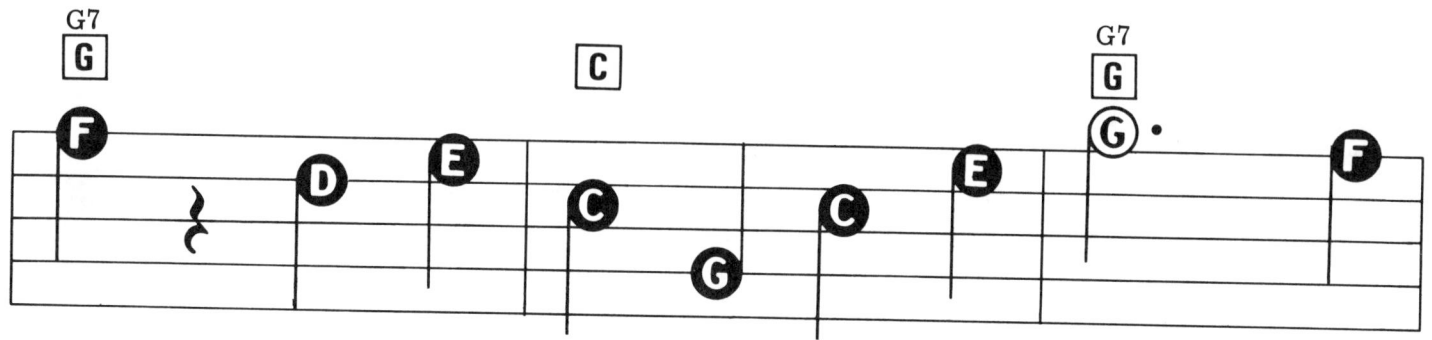
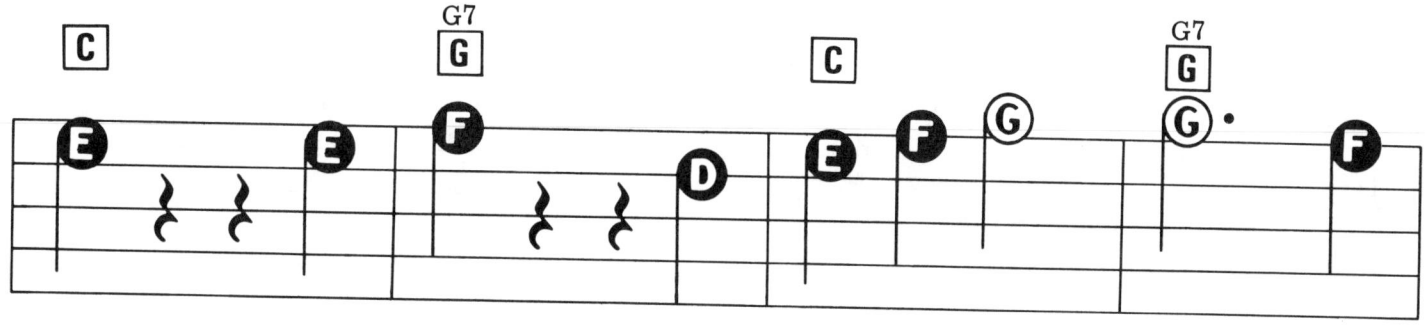
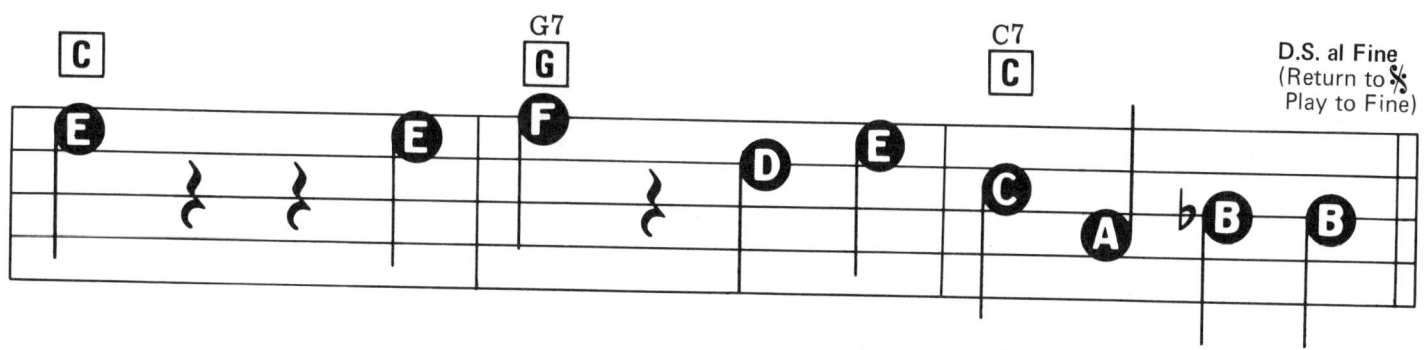

La Sorella

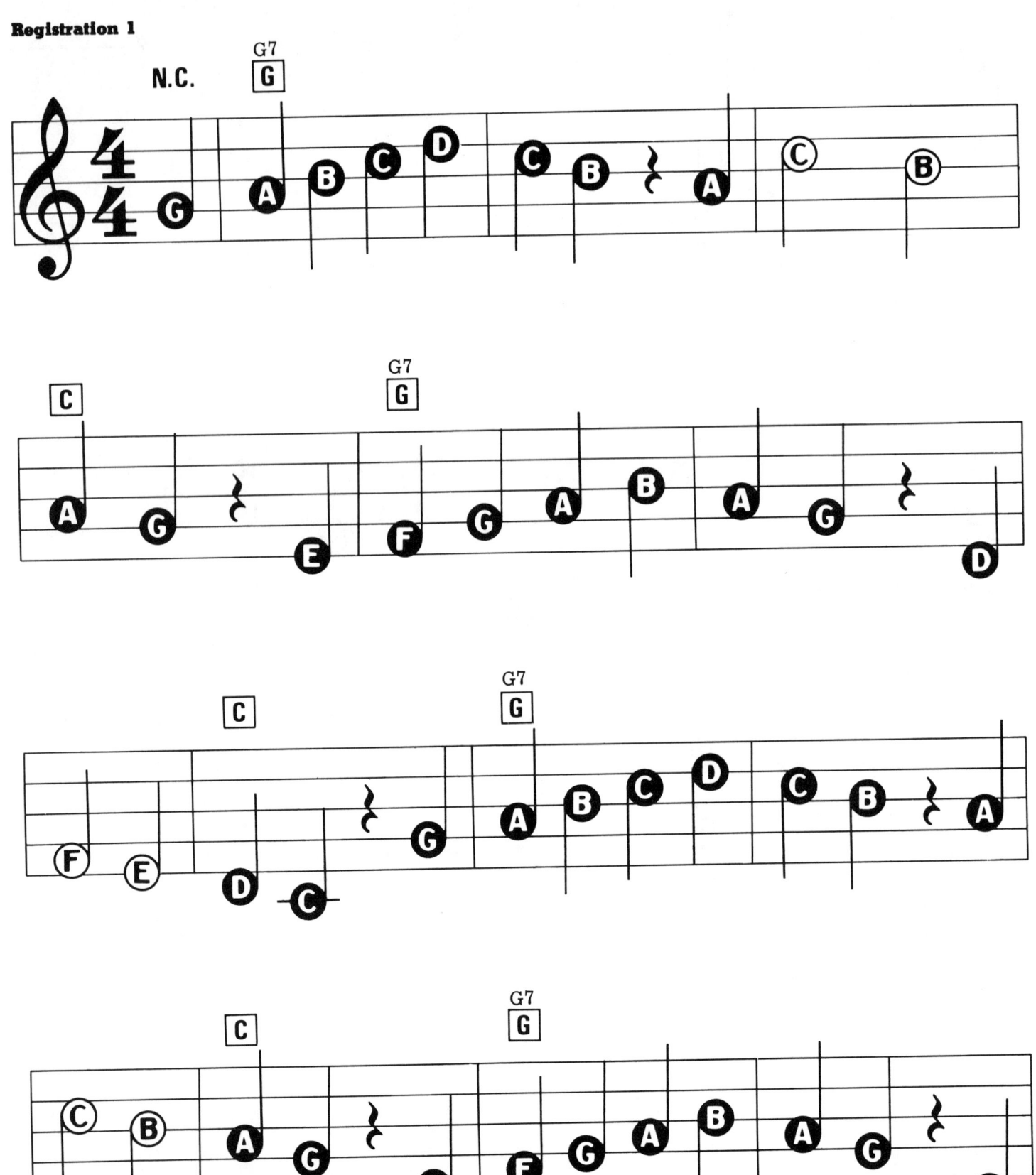

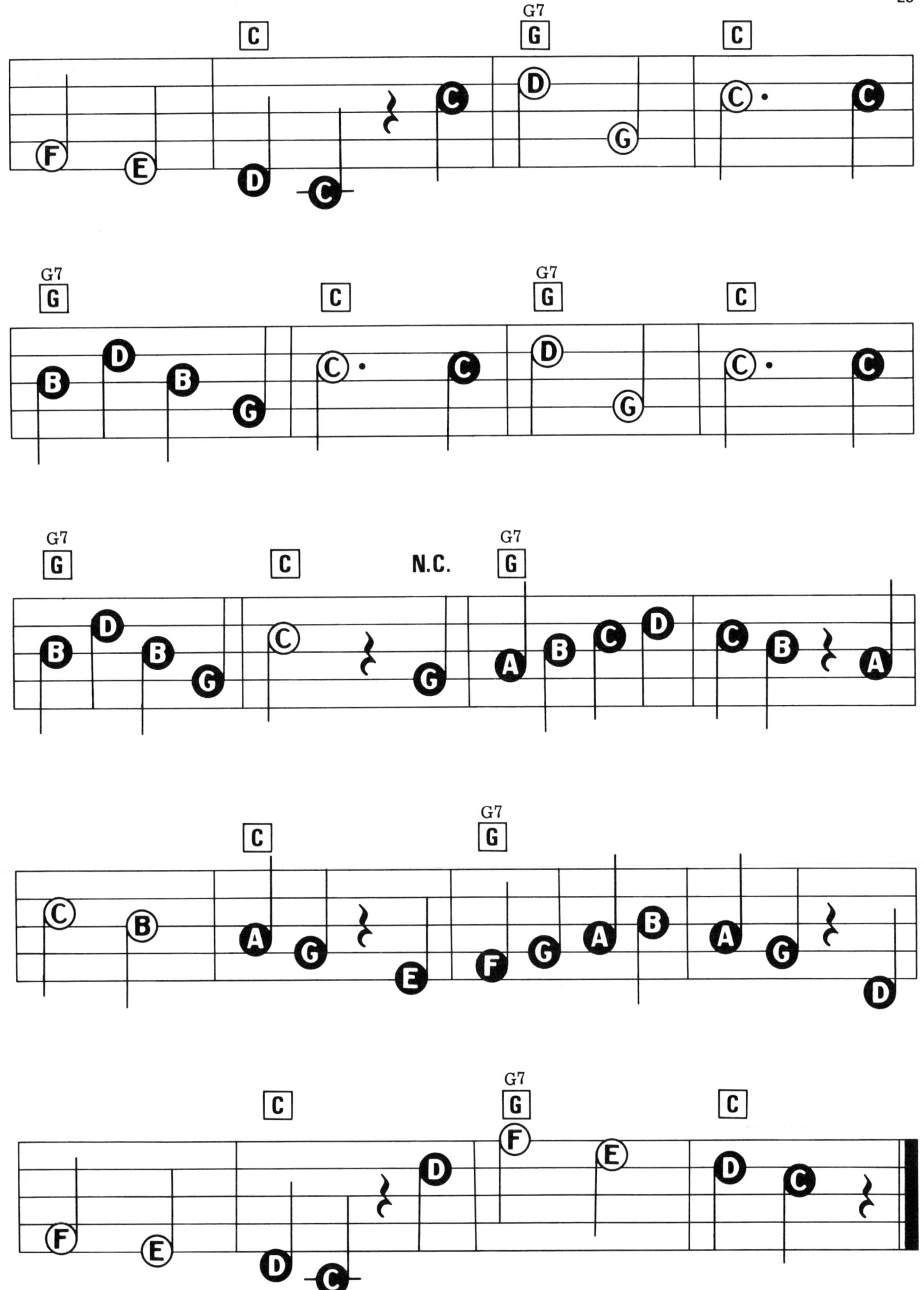

Liberty Bell March

Registration 3

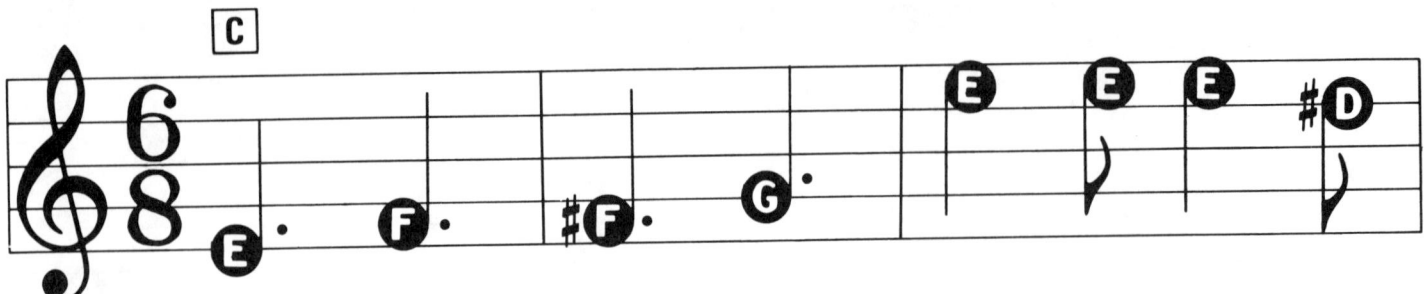

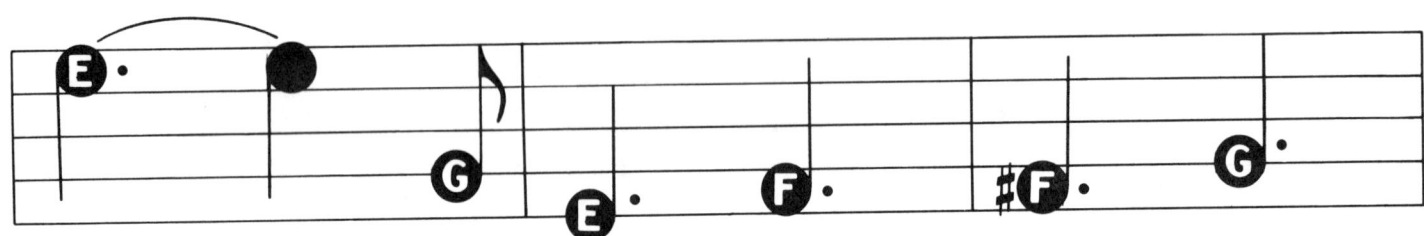

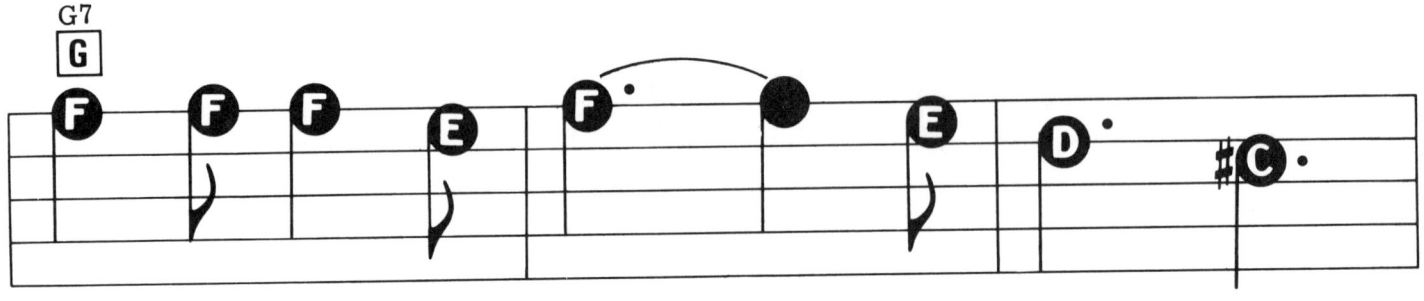

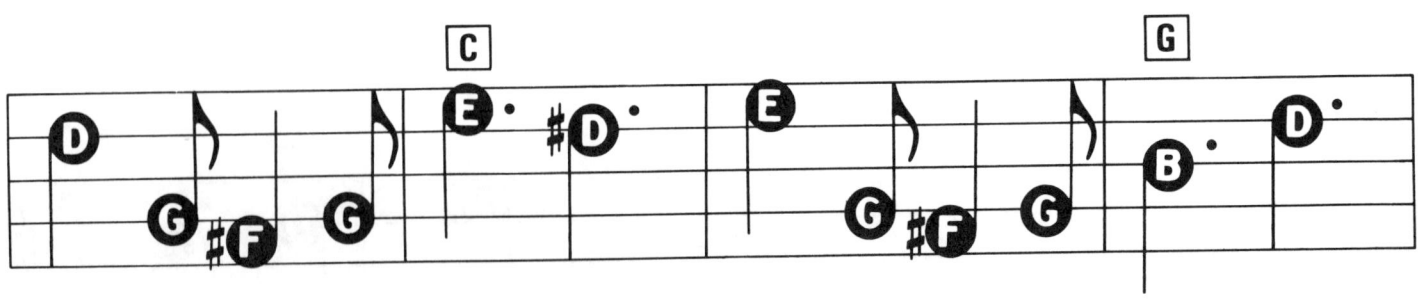

This arr. © Copyright 1976 by HAL LEONARD PUBLISHING CORPORATION, Winona, MN 55987
Made in U.S.A.   International Copyright Secured   All Rights Reserved

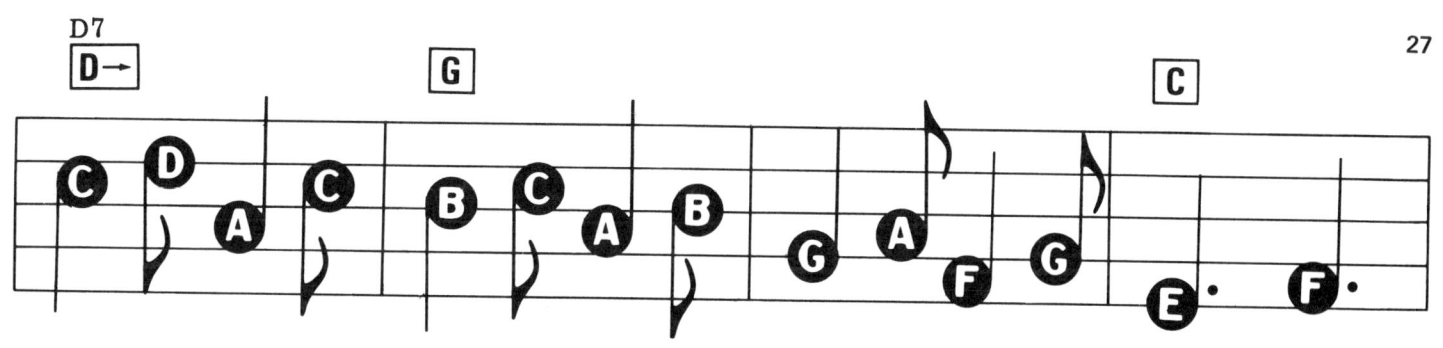
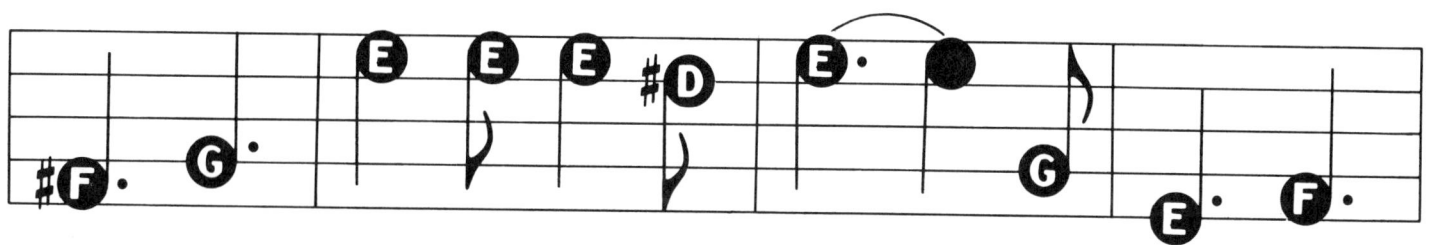
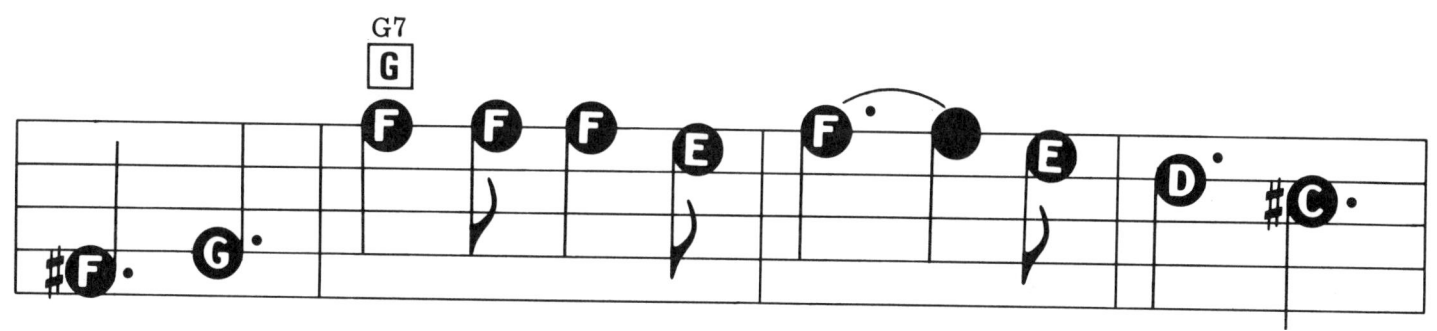
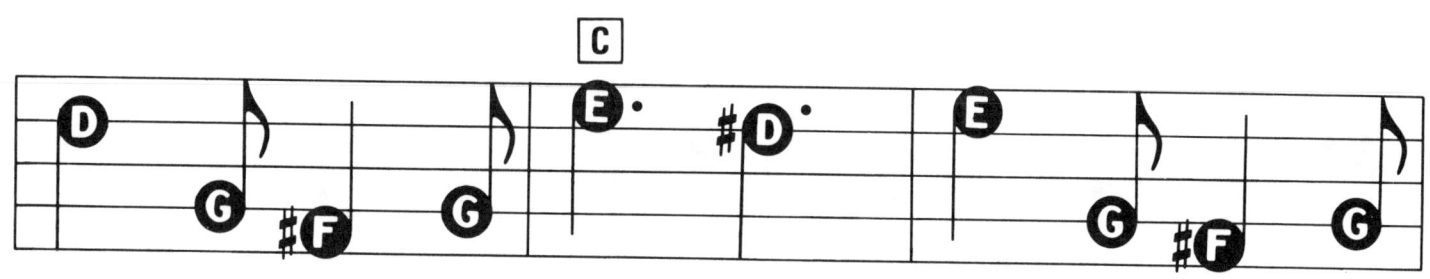
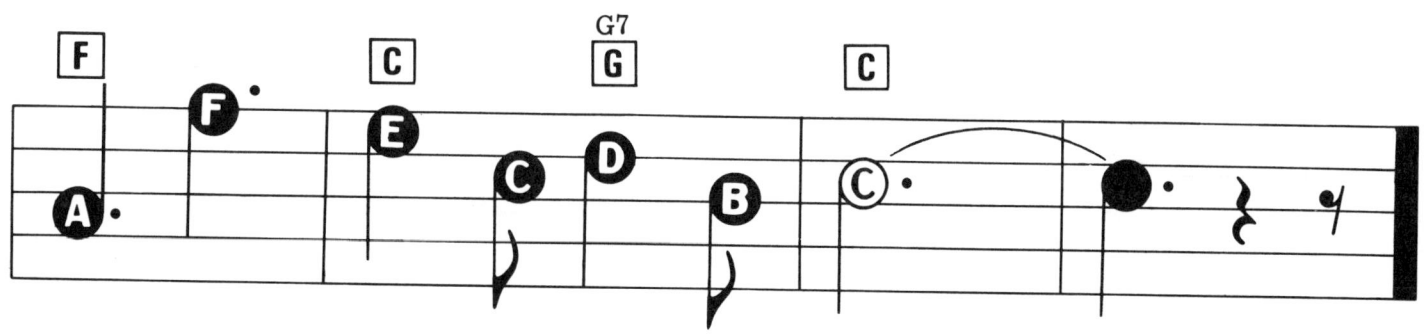

Lucia Polka

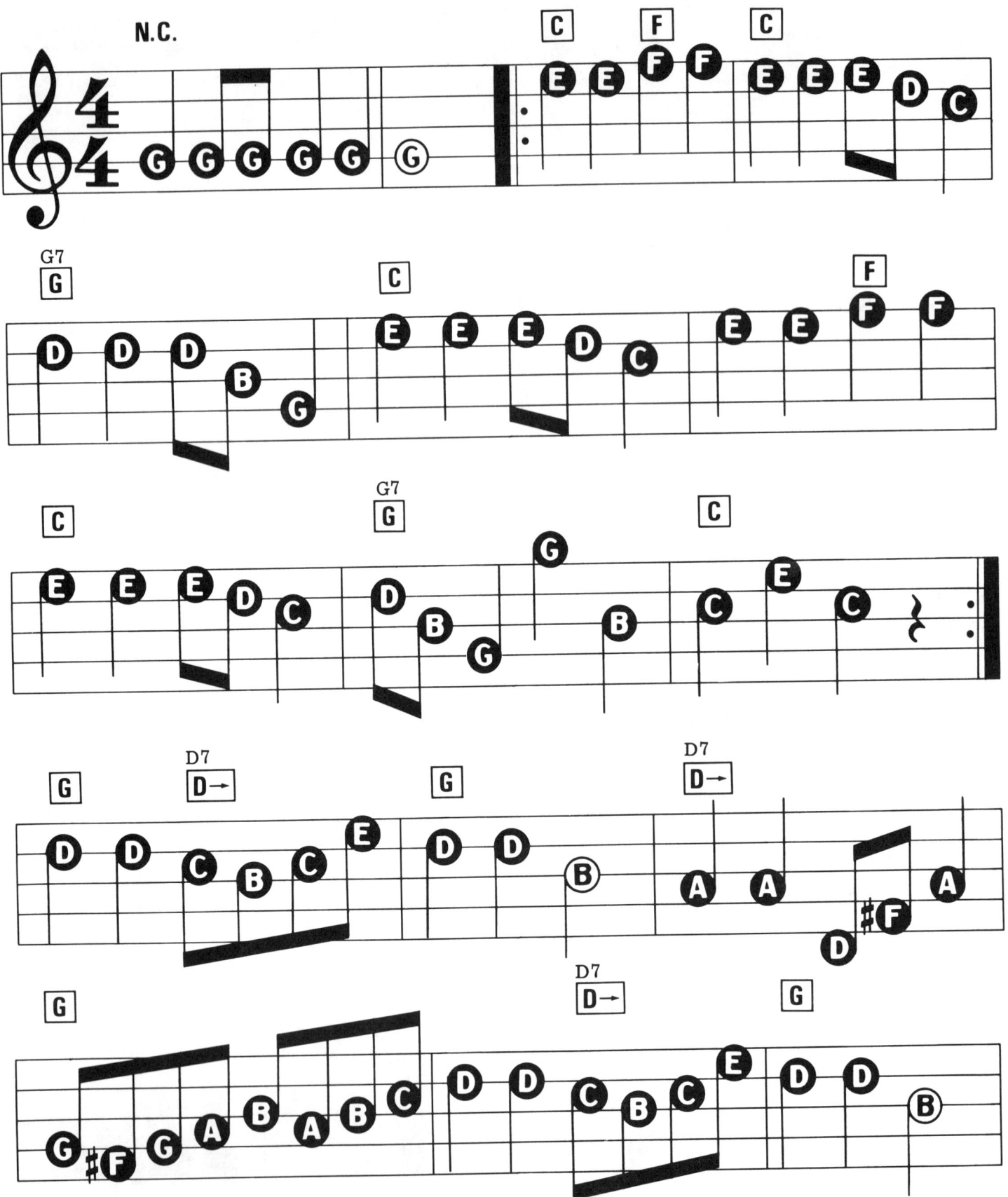

29

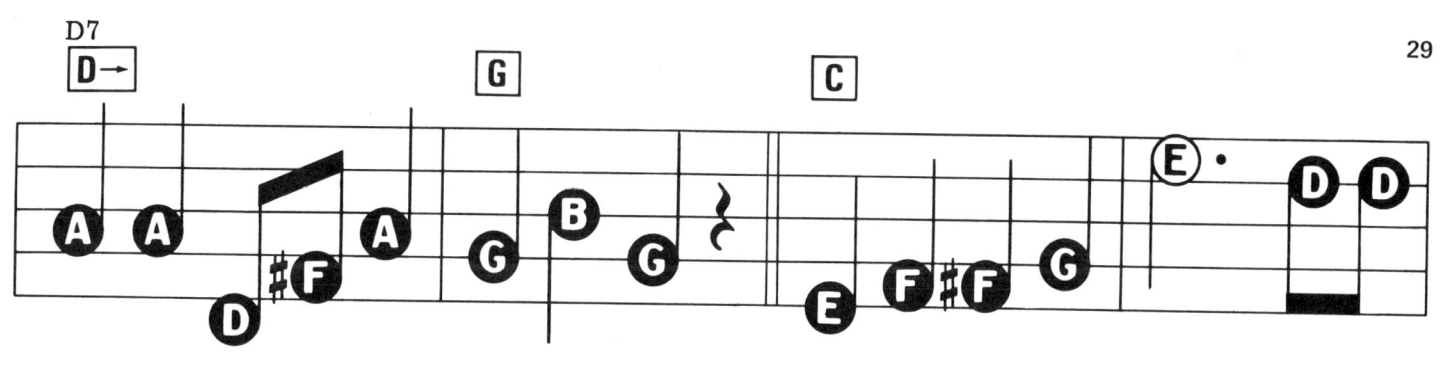
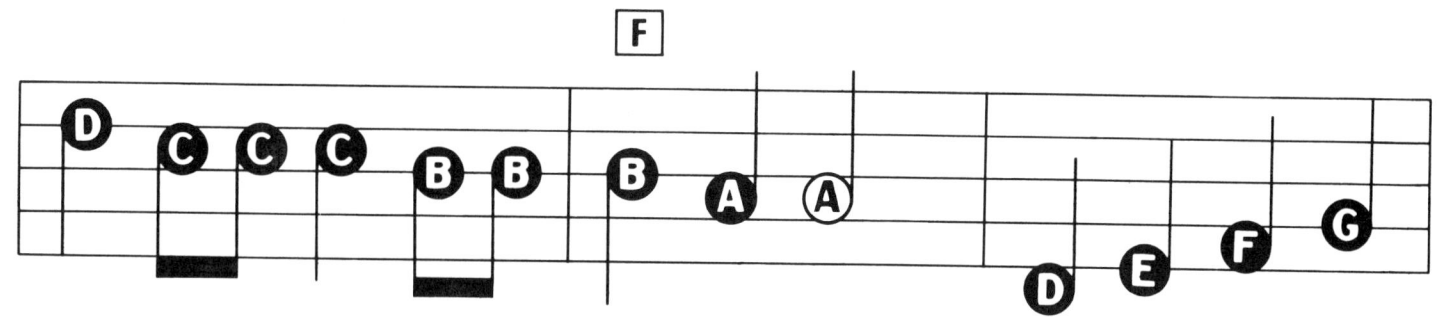
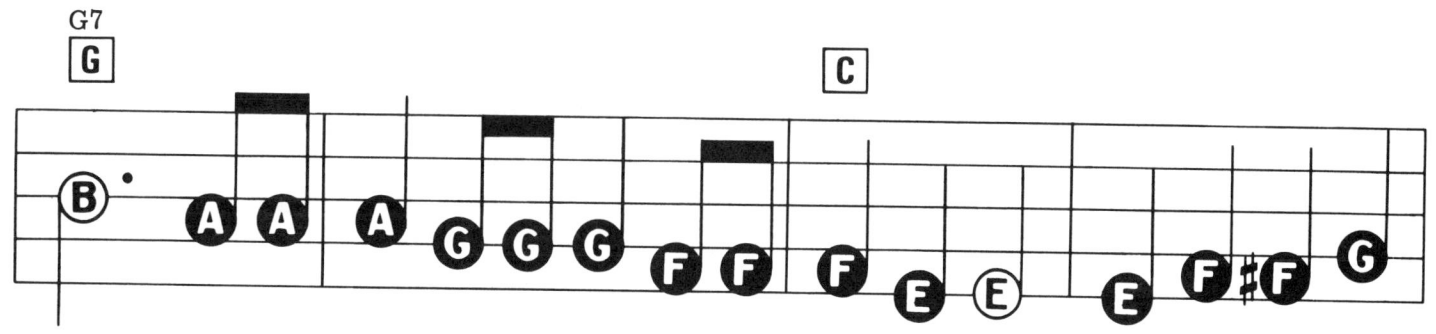
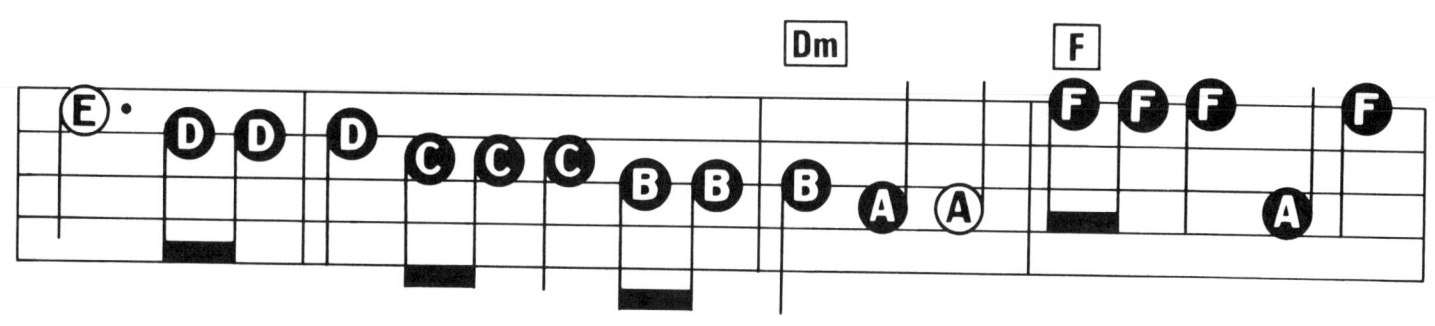
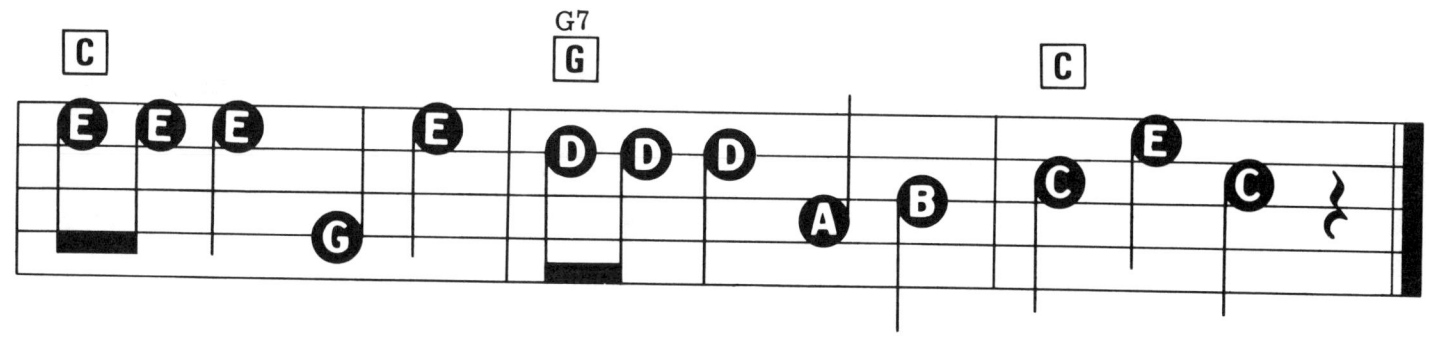

Mademoiselle From Armentiers

Registration 2

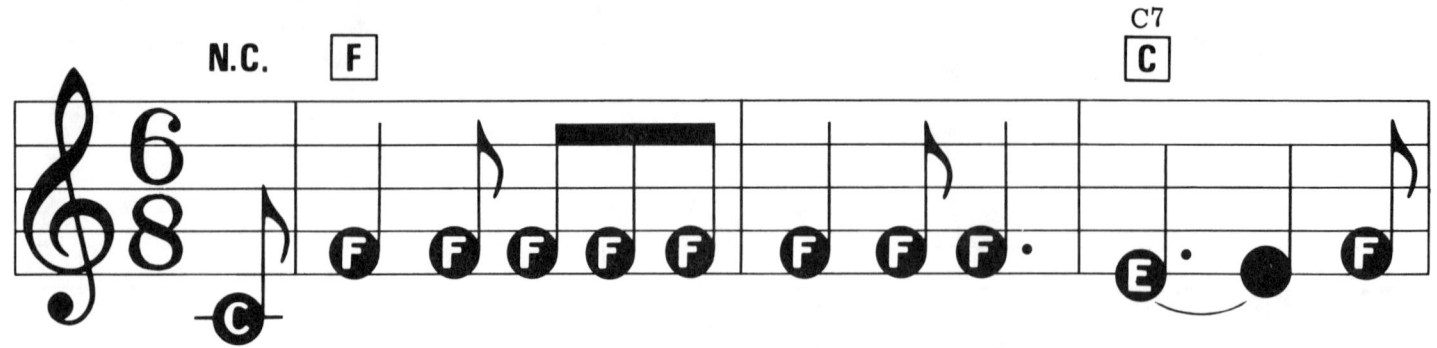
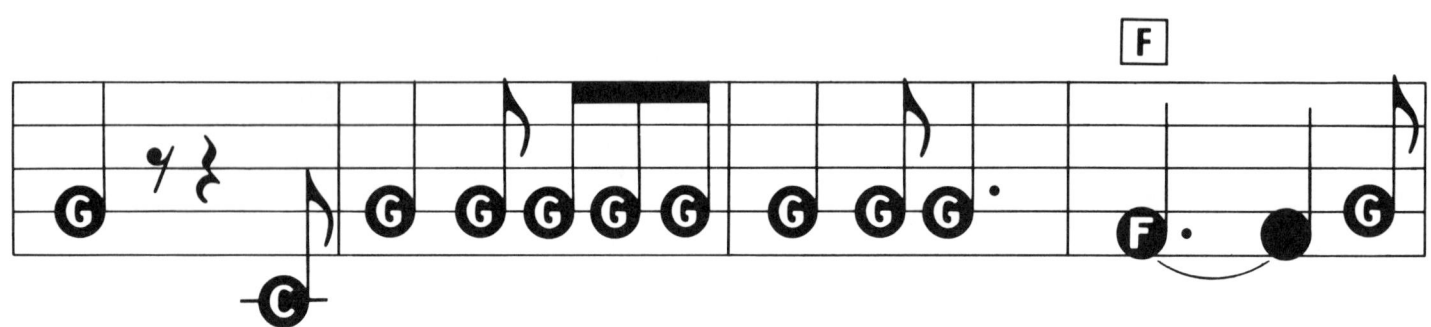
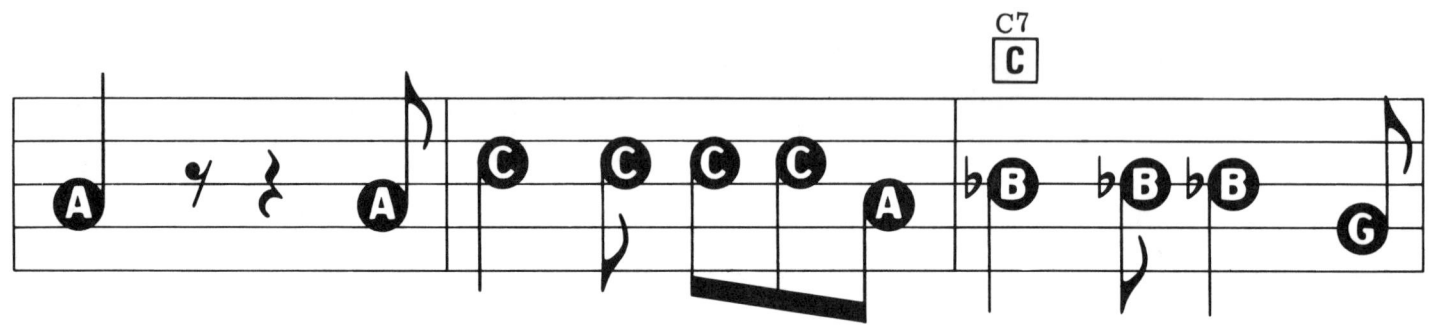
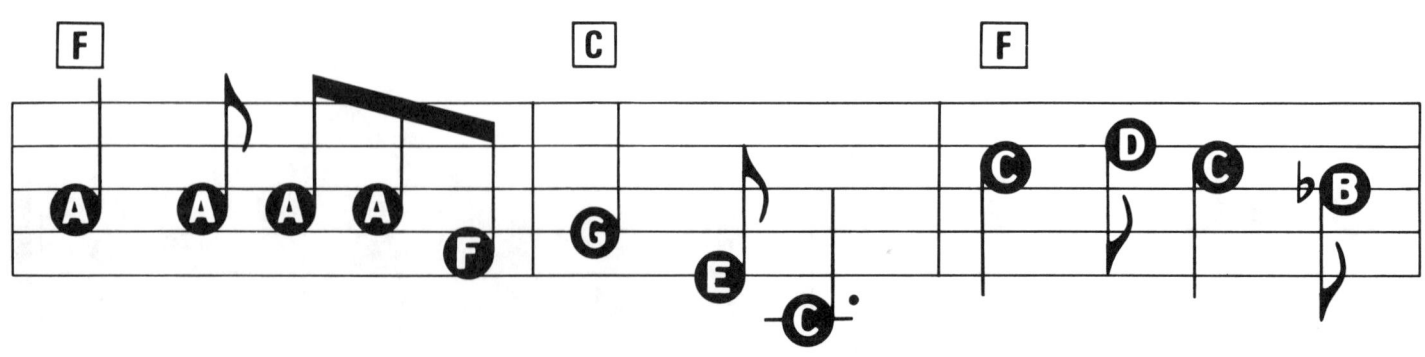

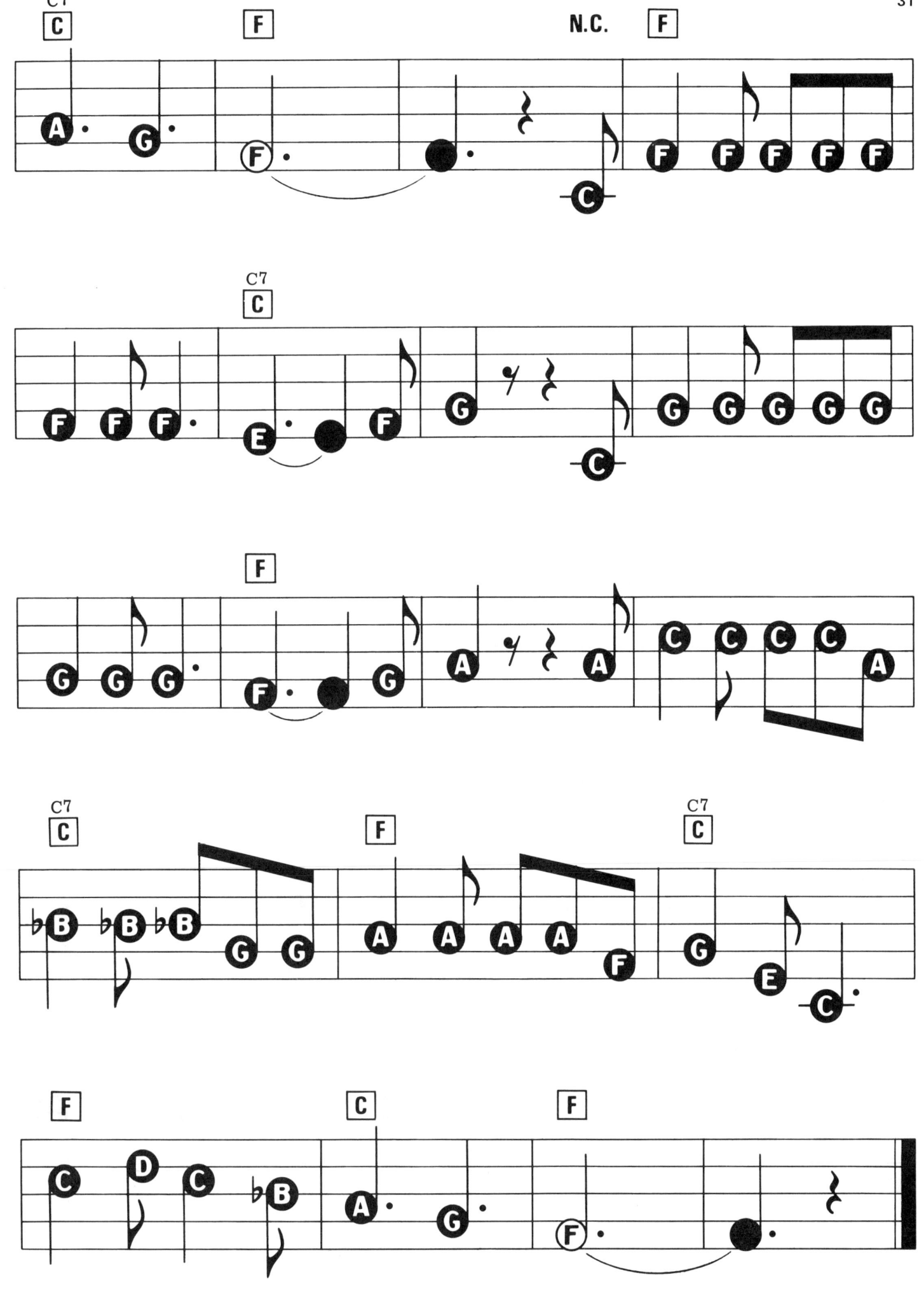

Martha Polka

Registration 4

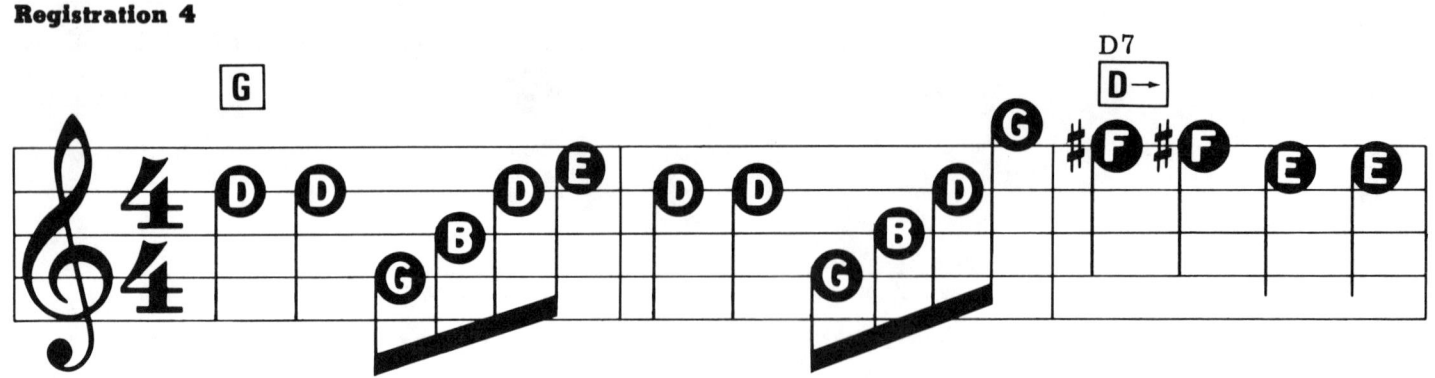
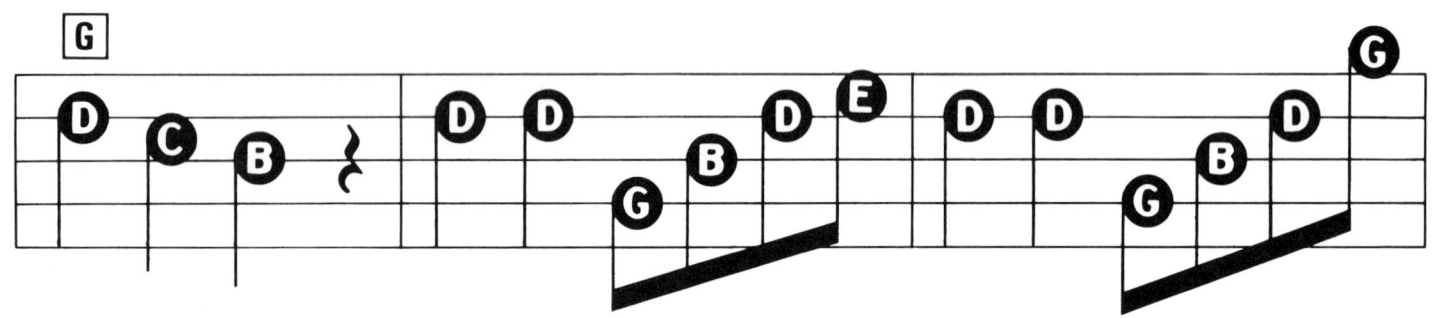
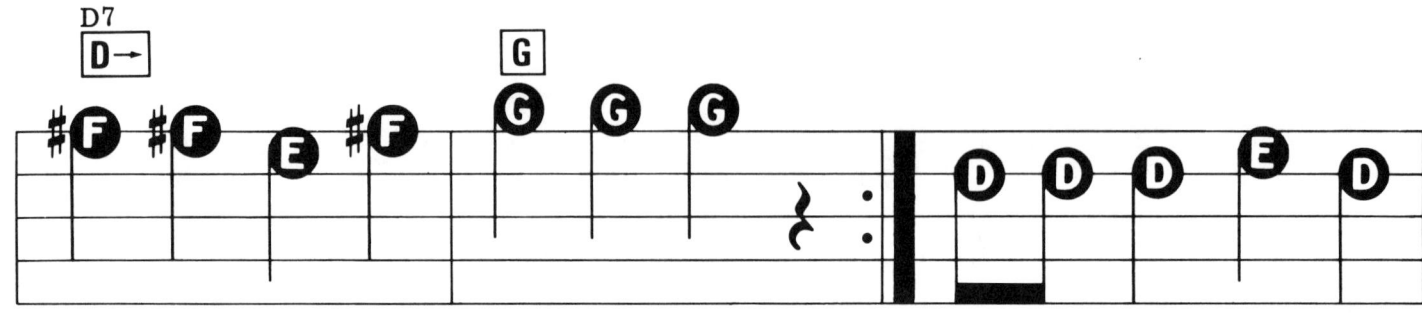
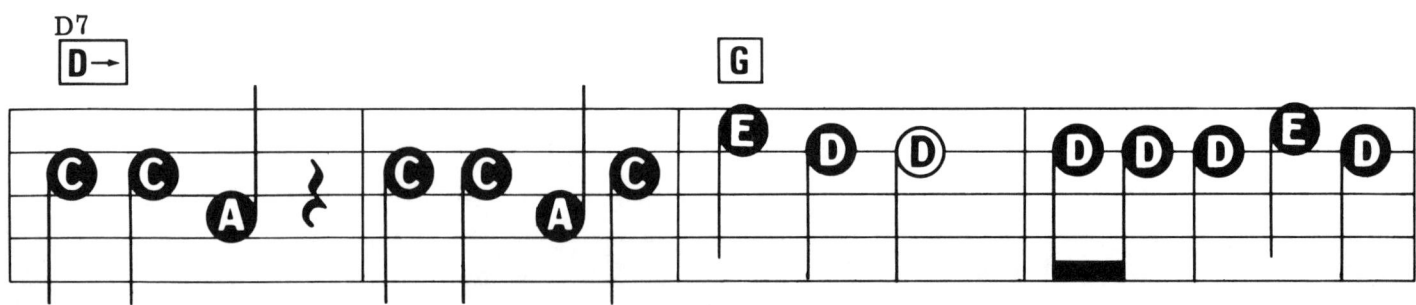

This arr. © Copyright 1976 by HAL LEONARD PUBLISHING CORPORATION, Winona, MN 55987
Made in U.S.A. International Copyright Secured All Rights Reserved

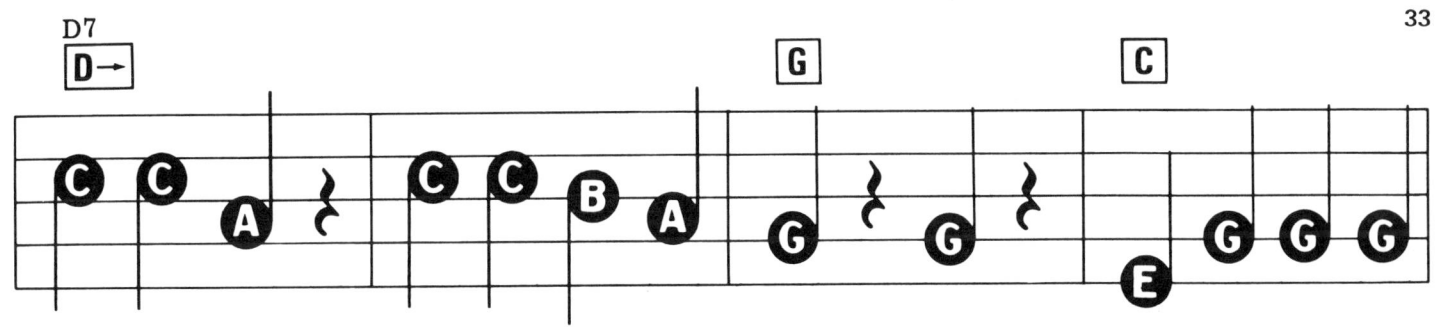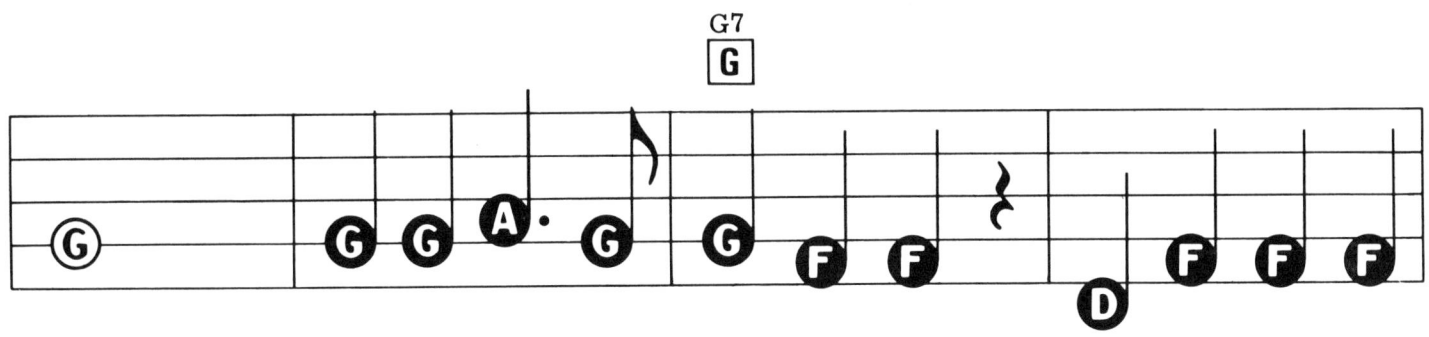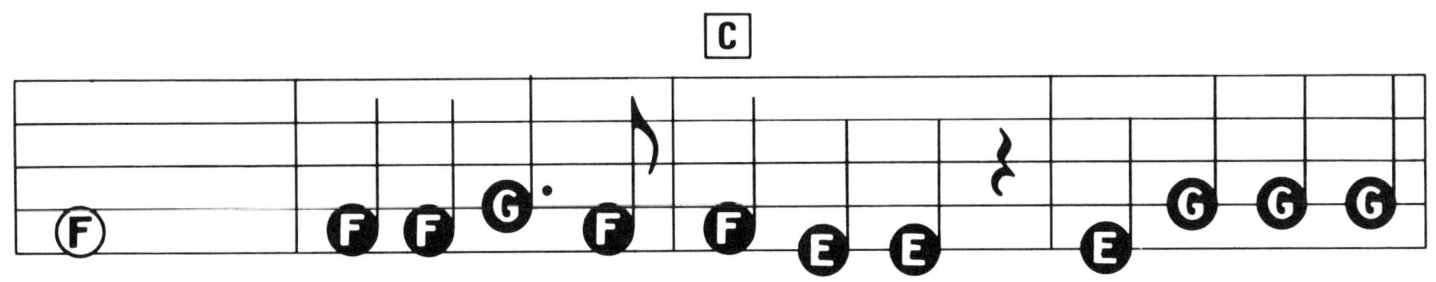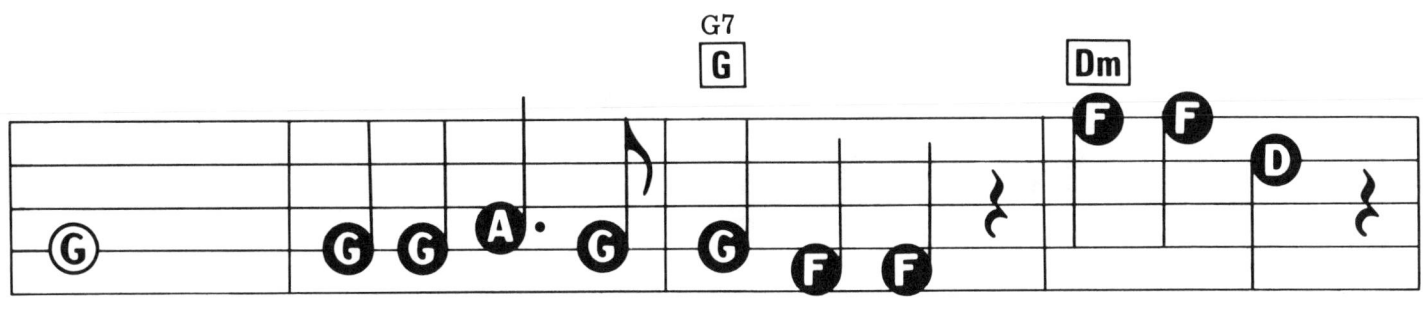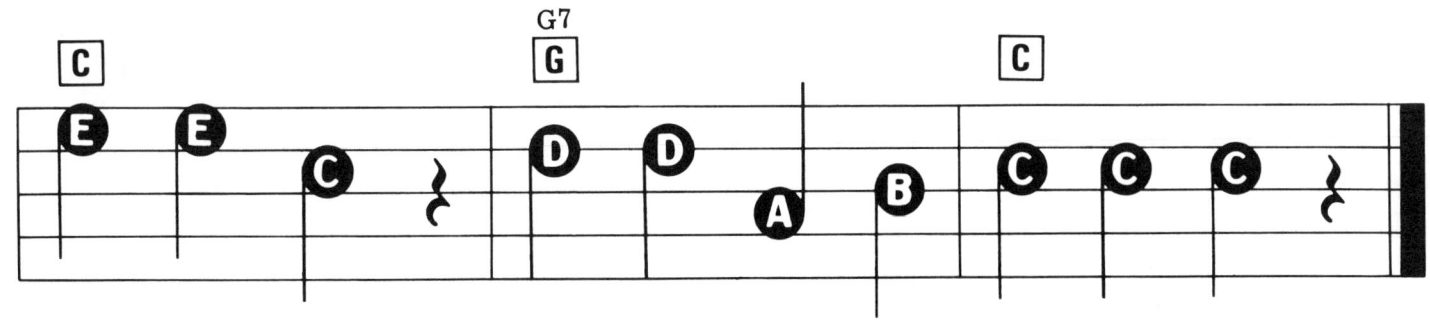

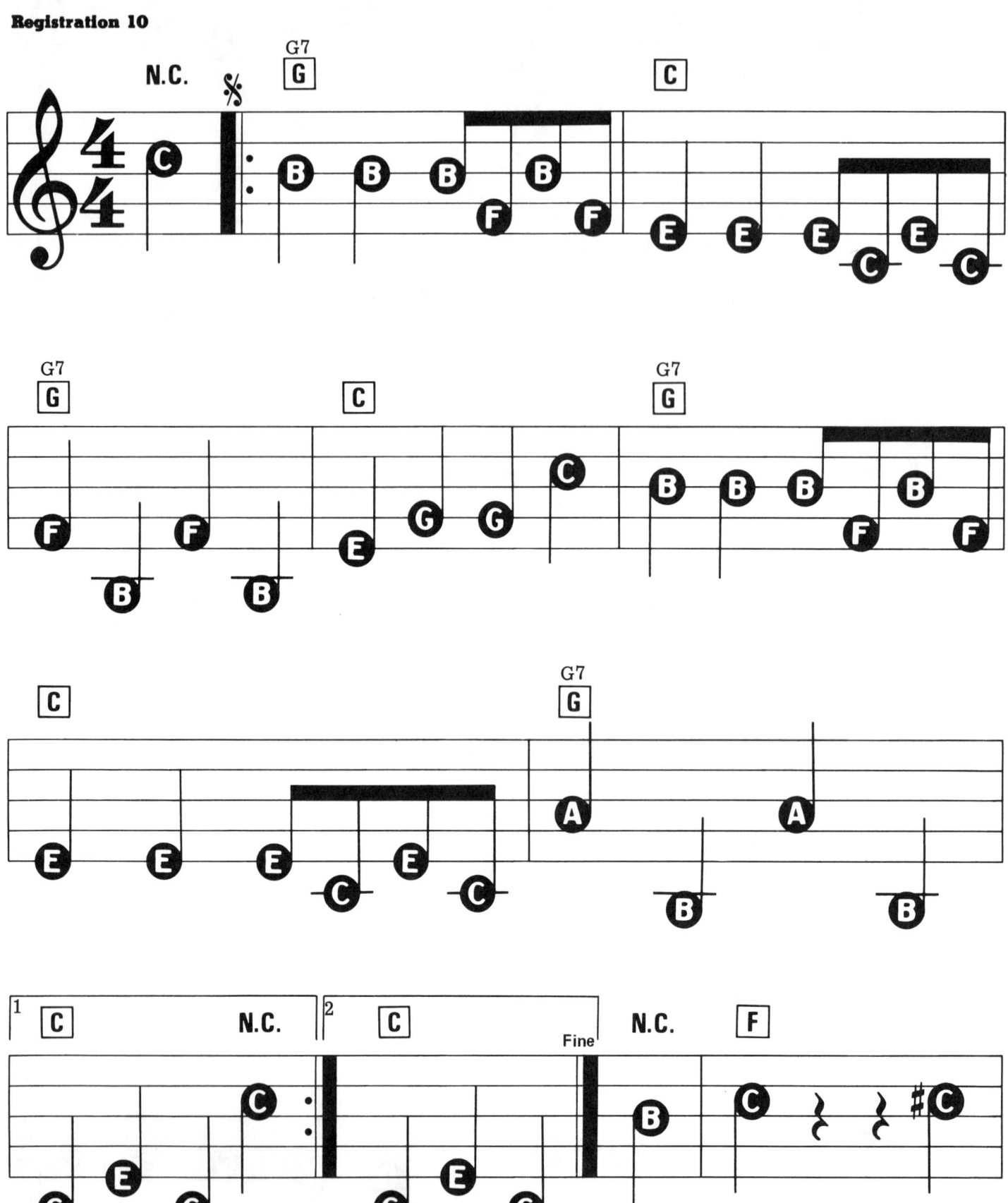

35

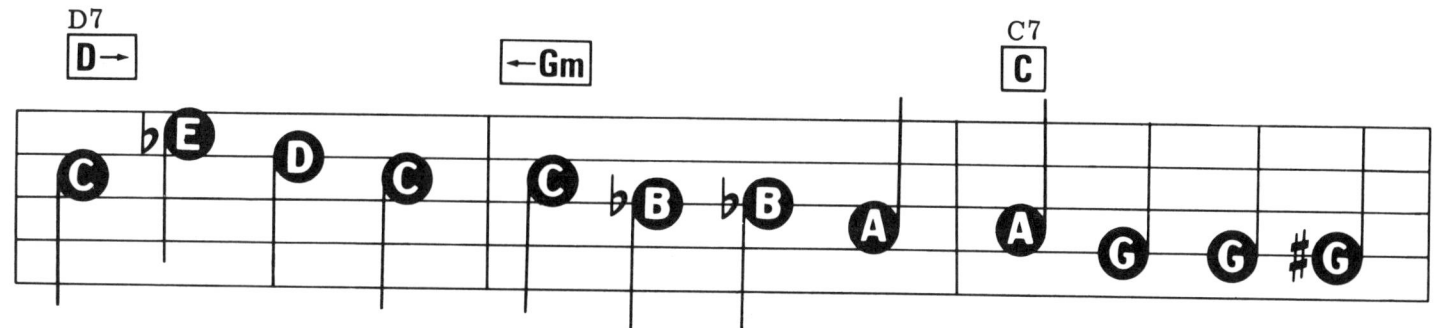
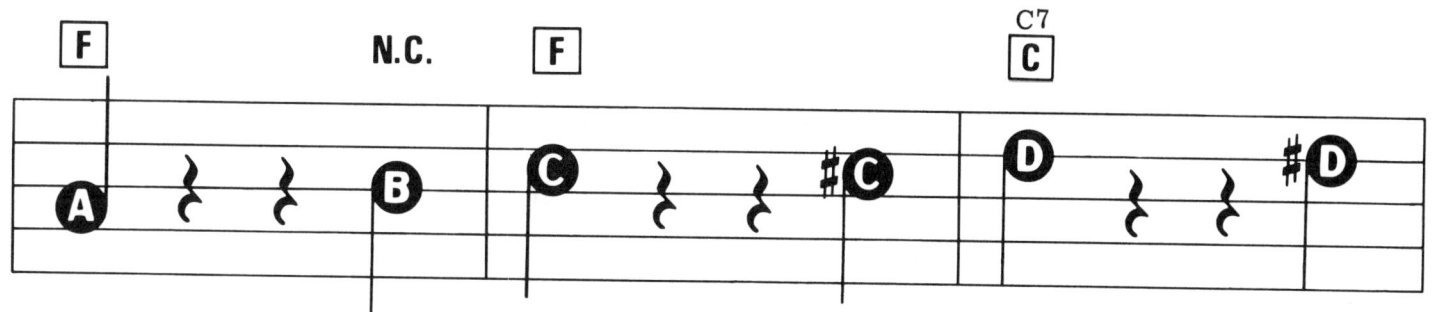
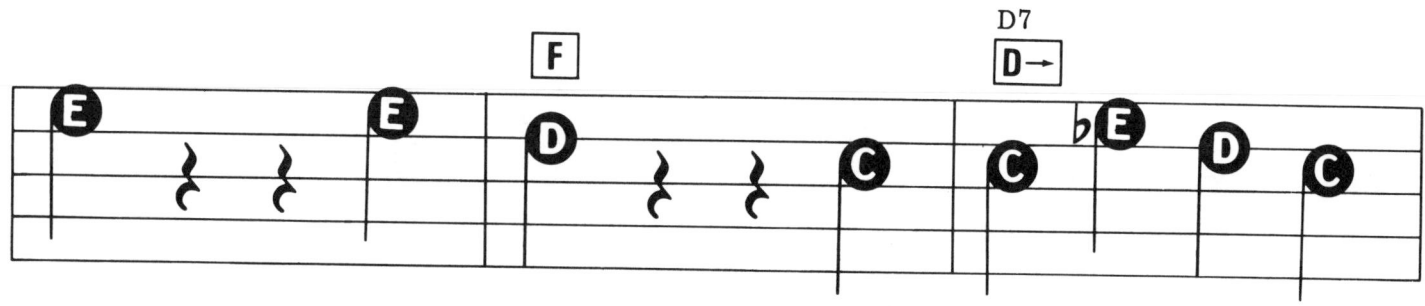
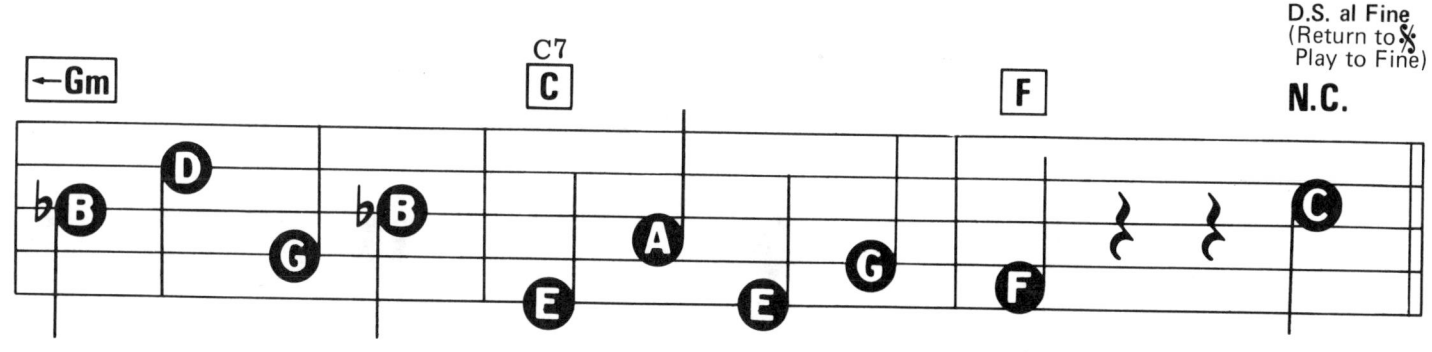

Semper Fidelis

Registration 5

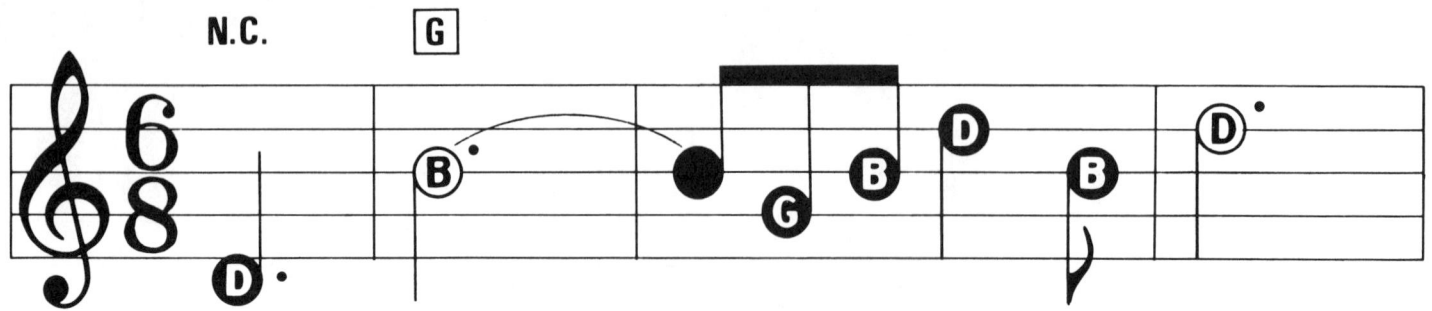
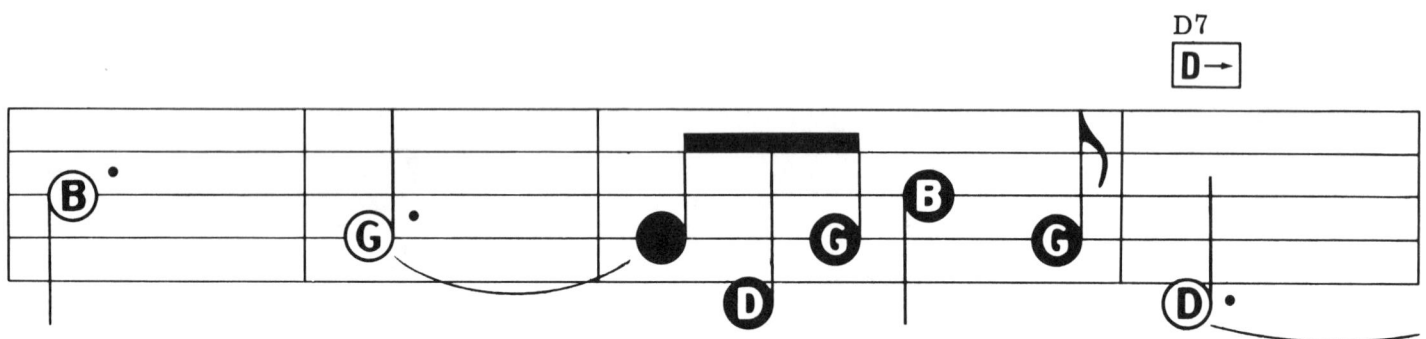
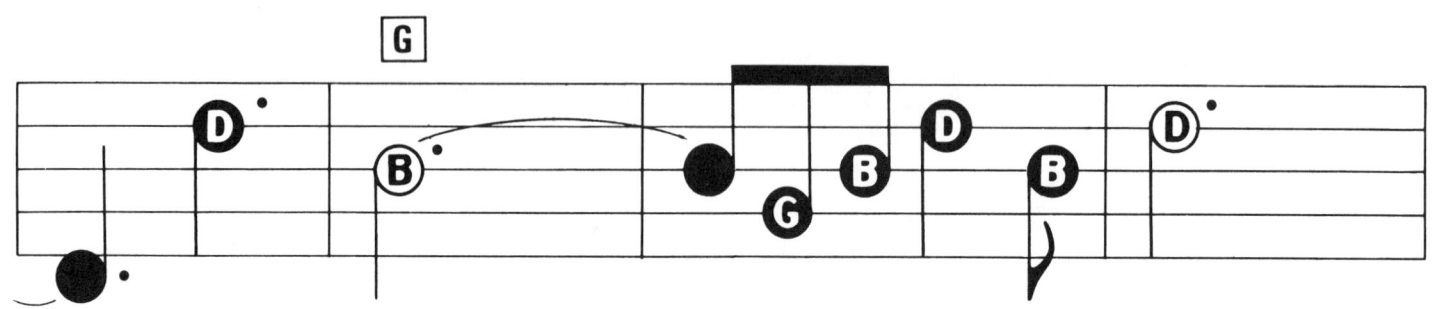
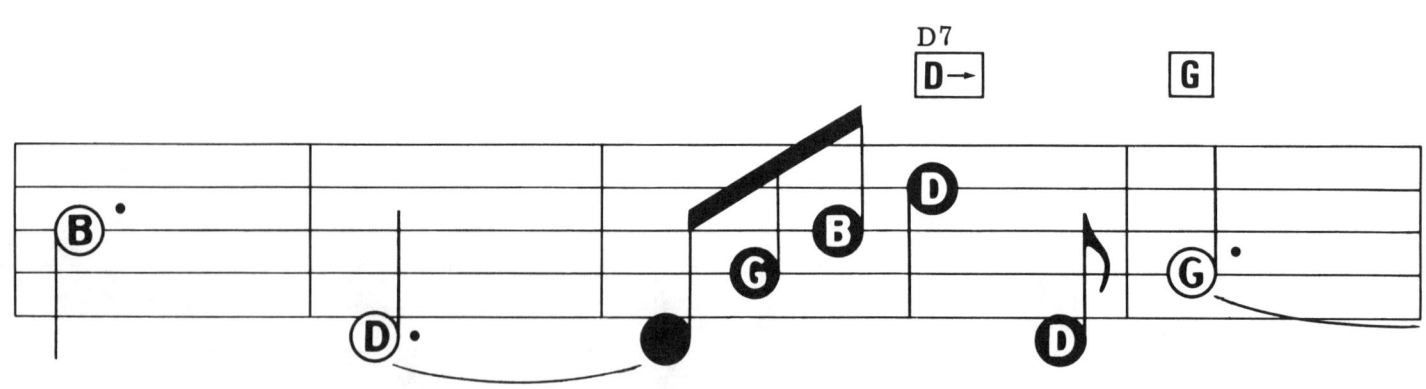

This arr. © Copyright 1976 by HAL LEONARD PUBLISHING CORPORATION, Winona, MN 55987
Made in U.S.A.   International Copyright Secured   All Rights Reserved

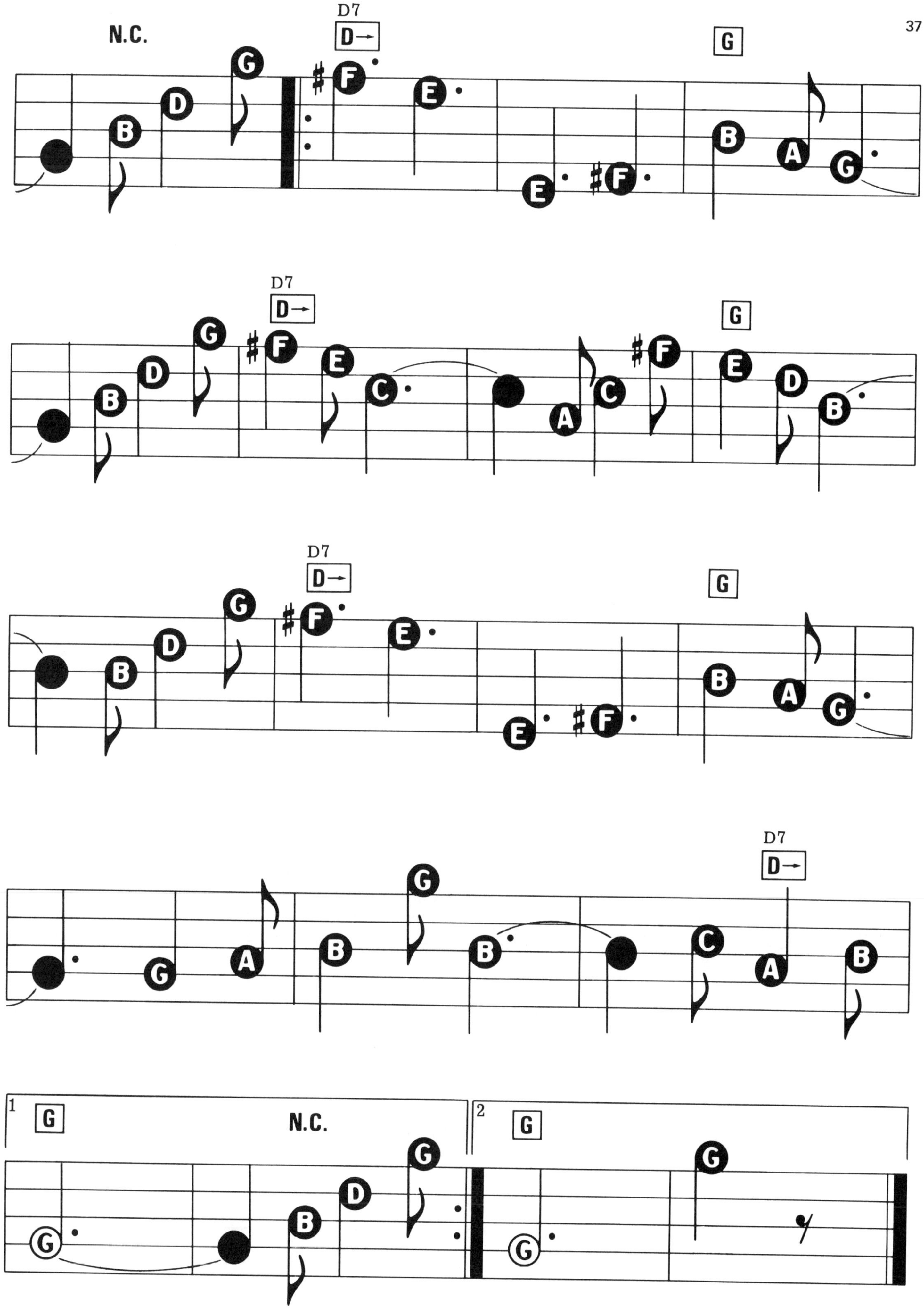
N.C.
D7
D→
G
D7
D→
G
D7
D→
G
D7
D→
1
G
N.C.
2
G

Sharpshooters March

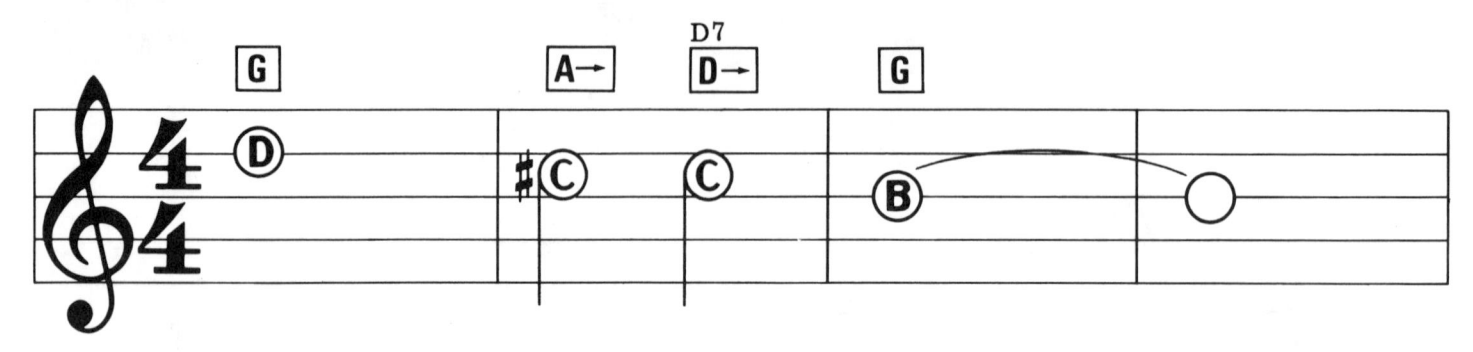

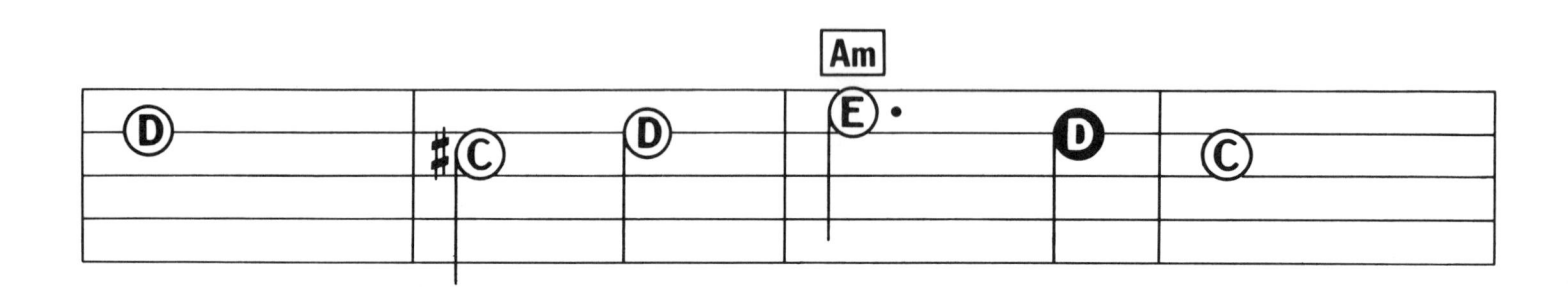

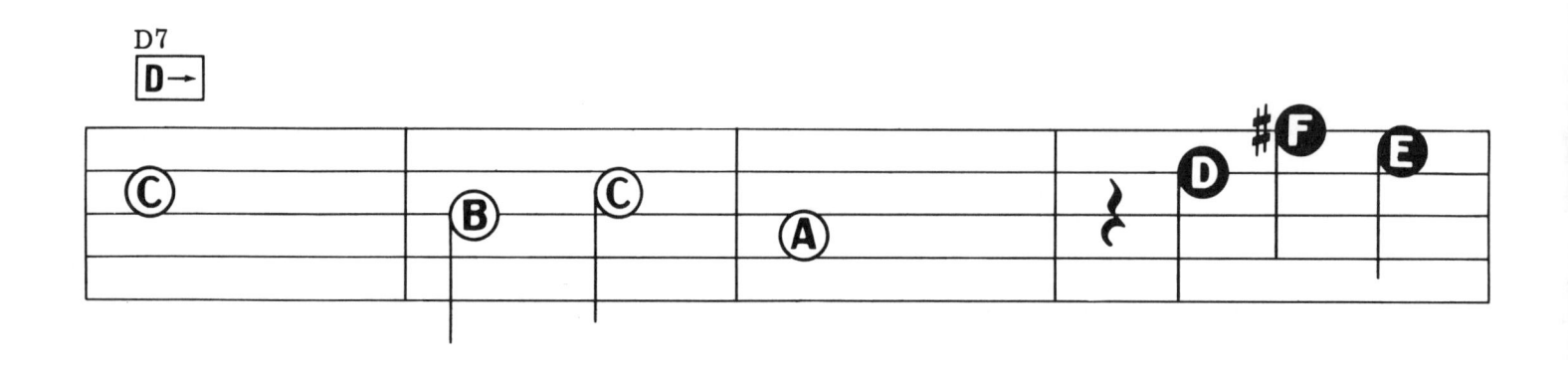

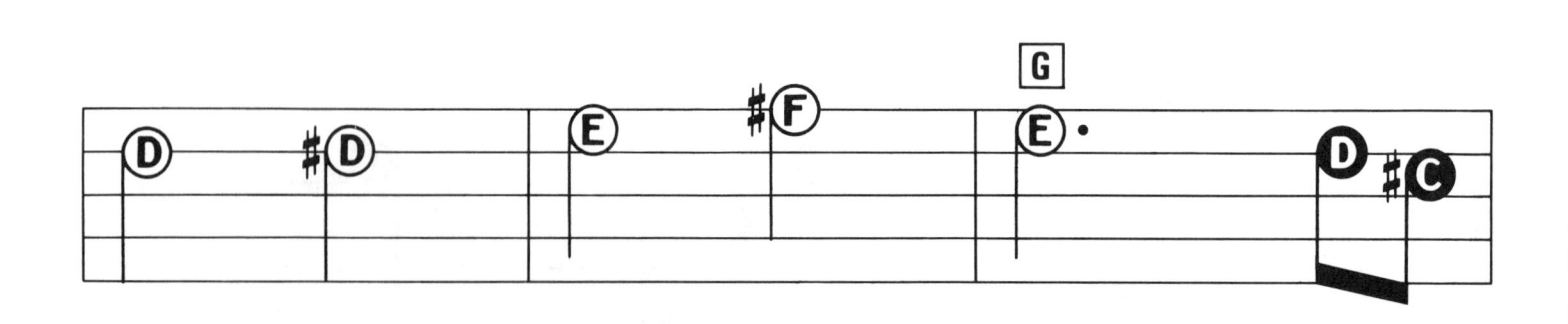

Registration 4

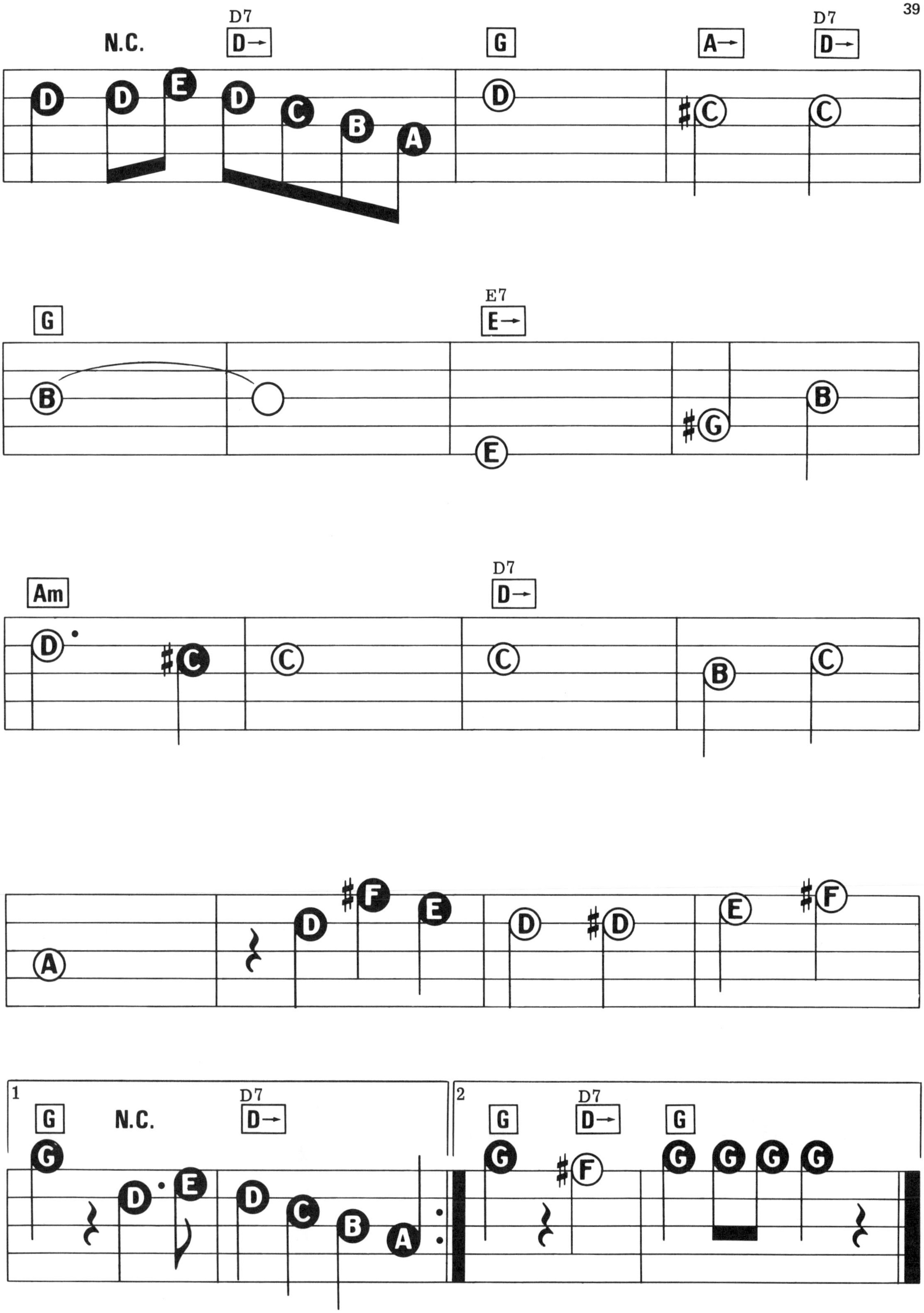
N.C.
D7 D→
G
A→
D7 D→
G
E7 E→
Am
D7 D→
1
G
N.C.
D7 D→
2
G
D7 D→
G

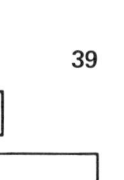

Thunder And Blazes

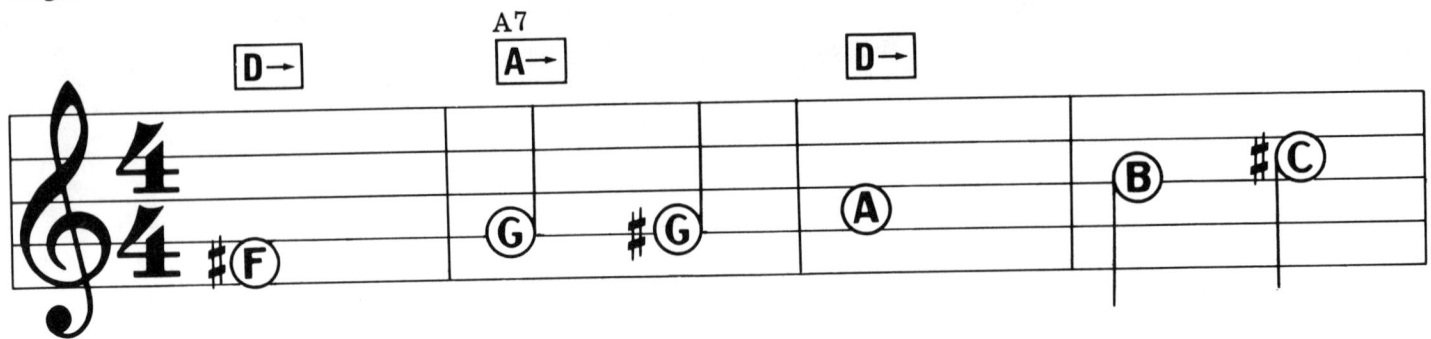

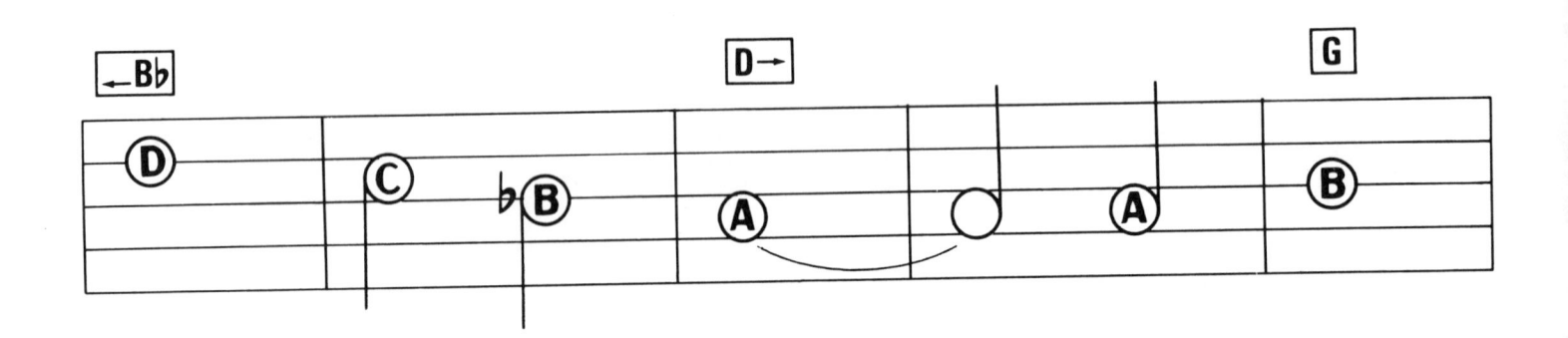

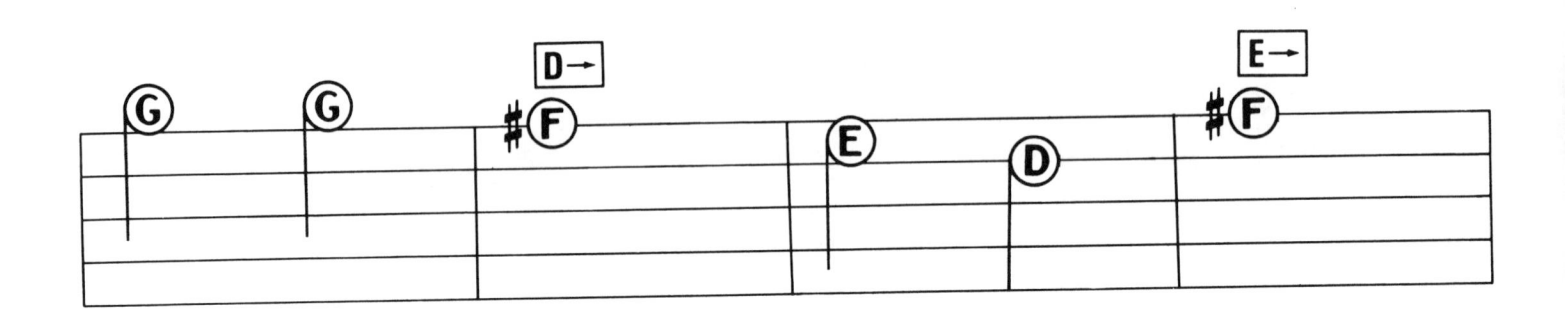

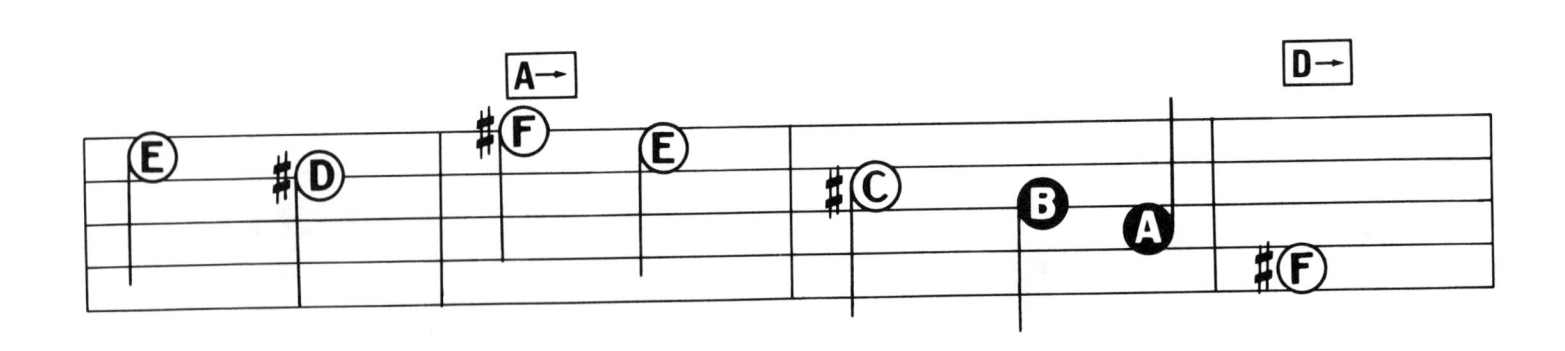

Registration 5

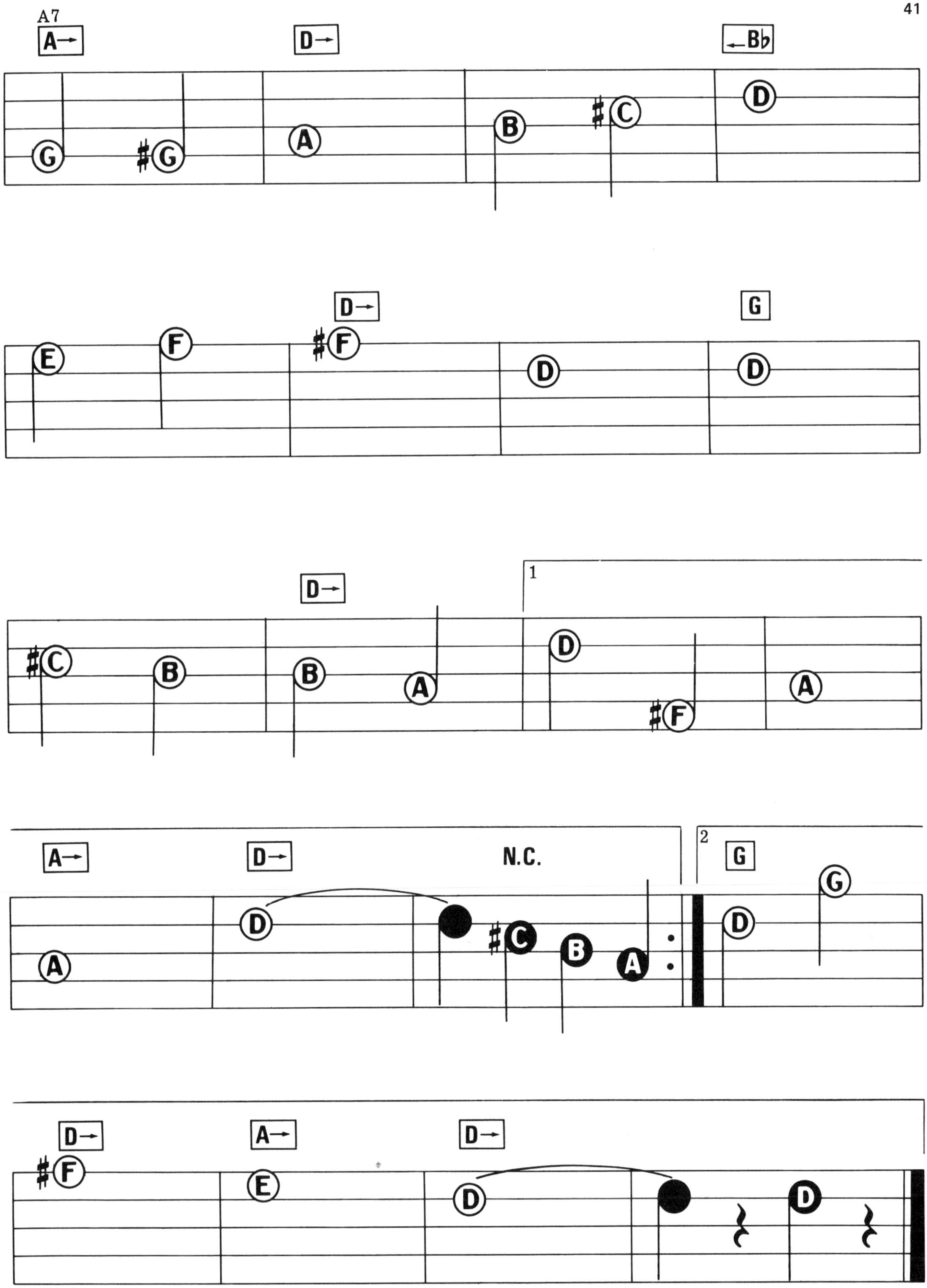
A7
A→
D→
←B♭
D→
G
D→
1
A→
D→
N.C.
2
G
D→
A→
D→

Tinker Polka

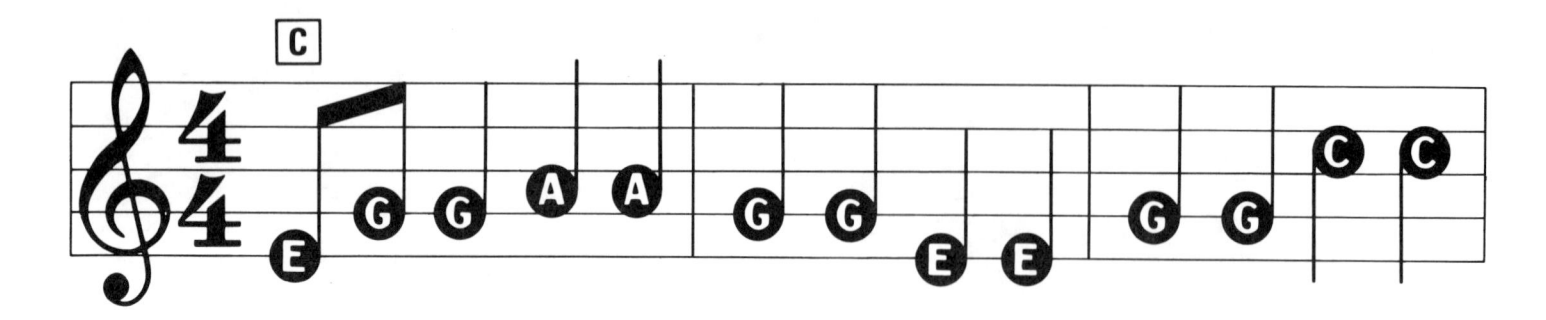

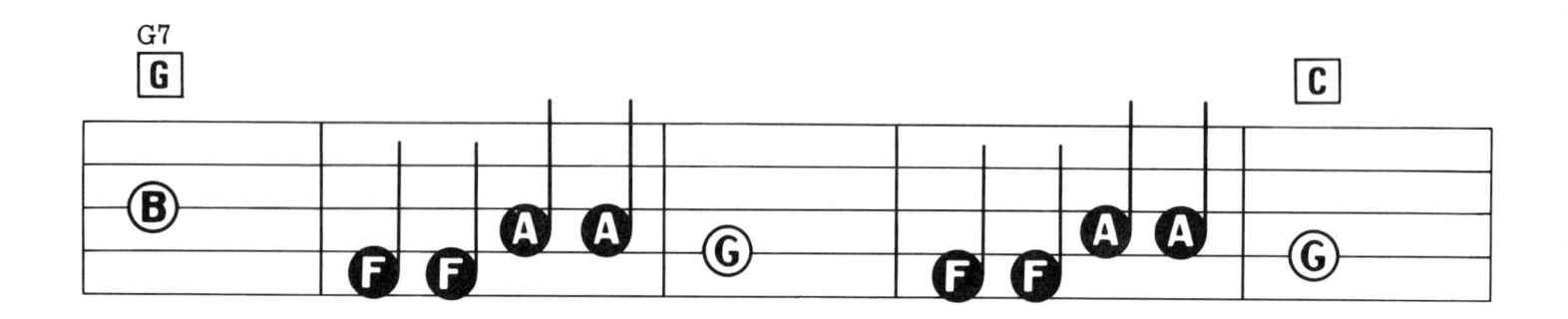

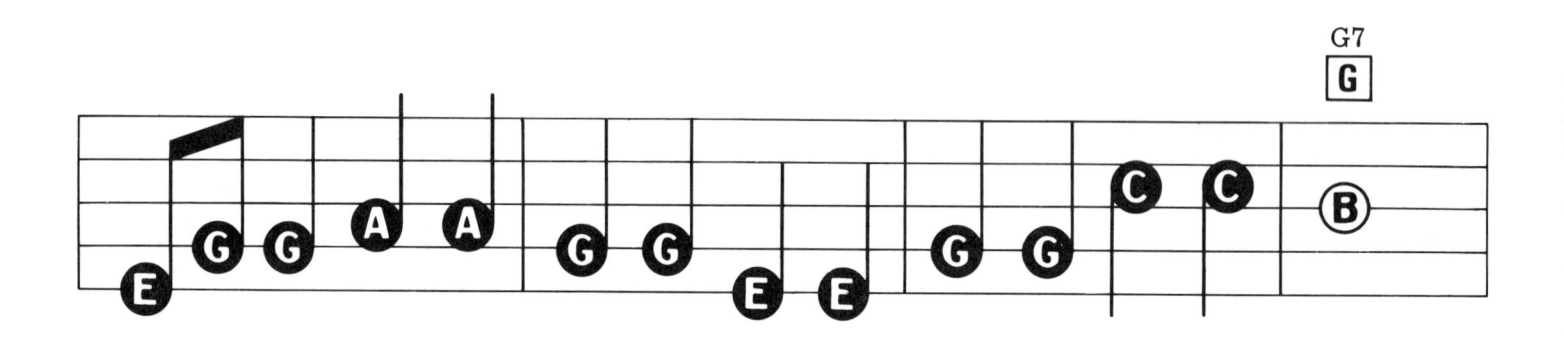

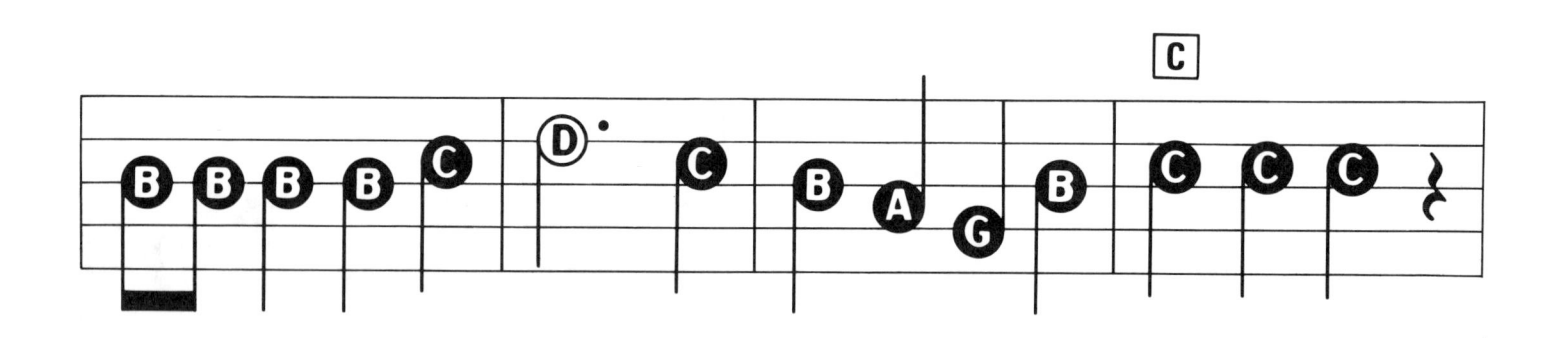

Registration 3

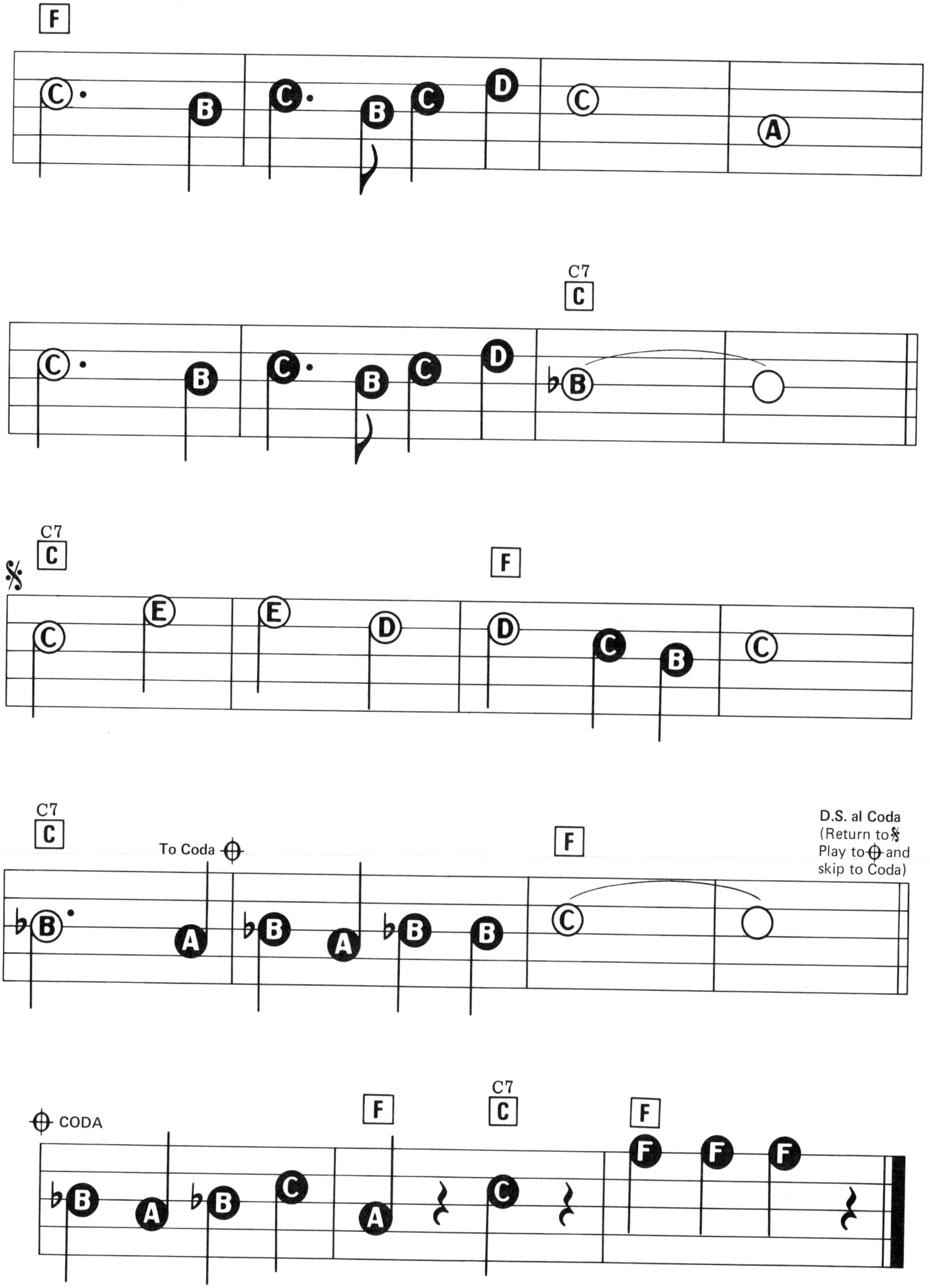

F
C7
C
C7
C
F
C7
C
To Coda
F
D.S. al Coda
(Return to 𝄋
Play to ⊕ and
skip to Coda)
⊕ CODA
F
C7
C
F

Toreador Song

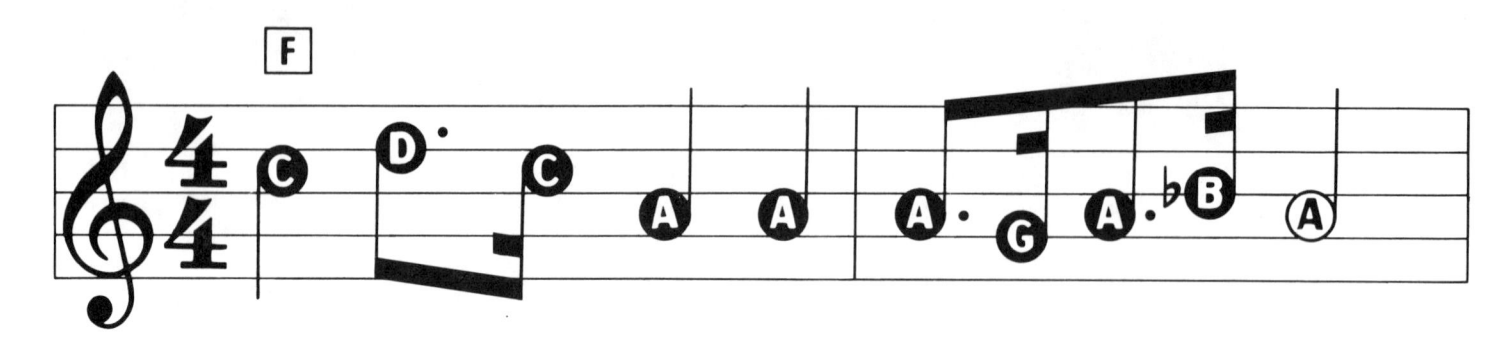

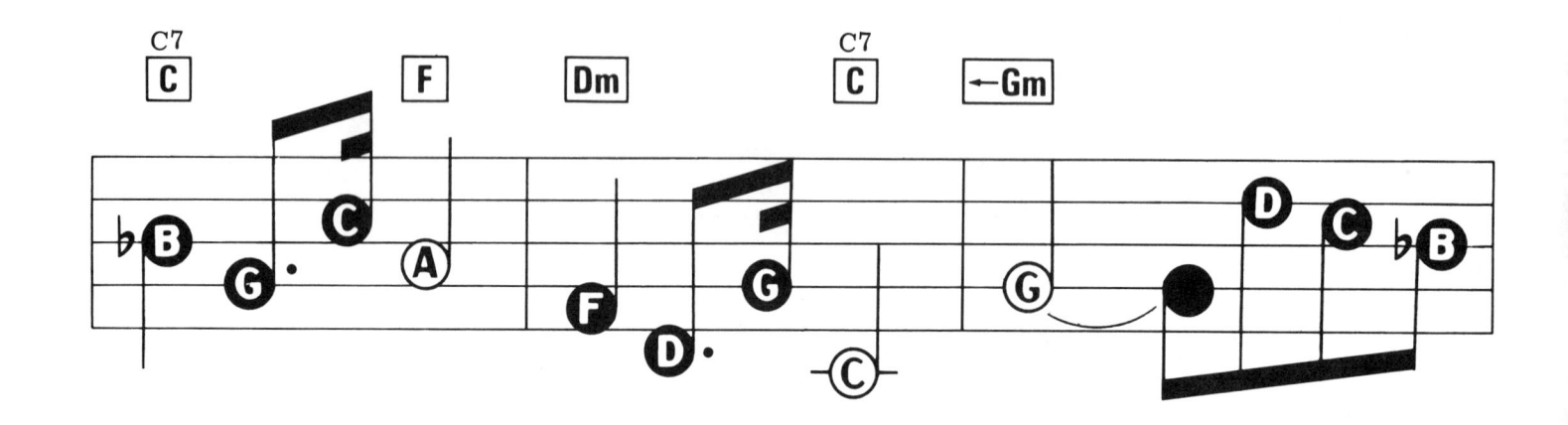

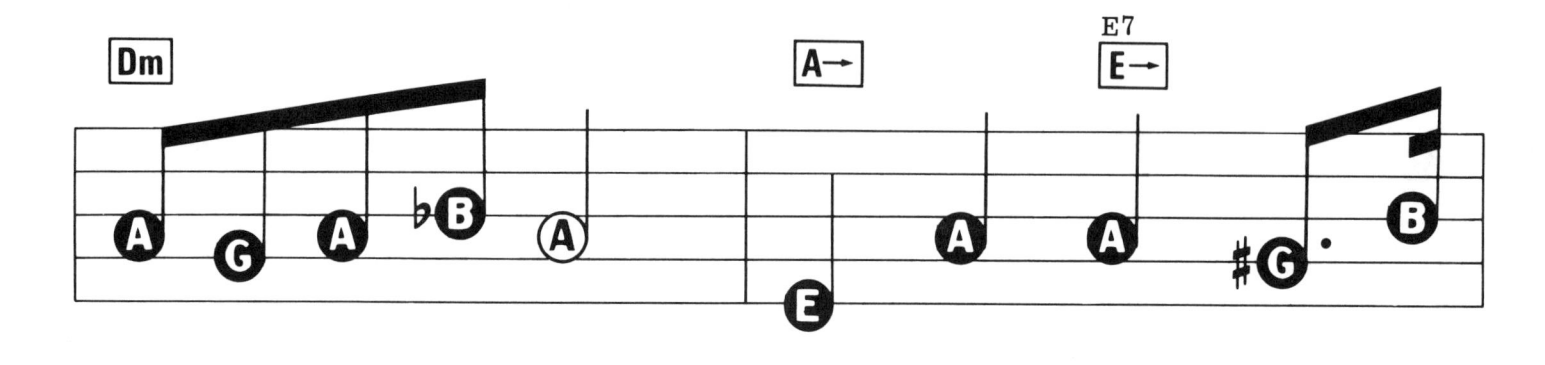

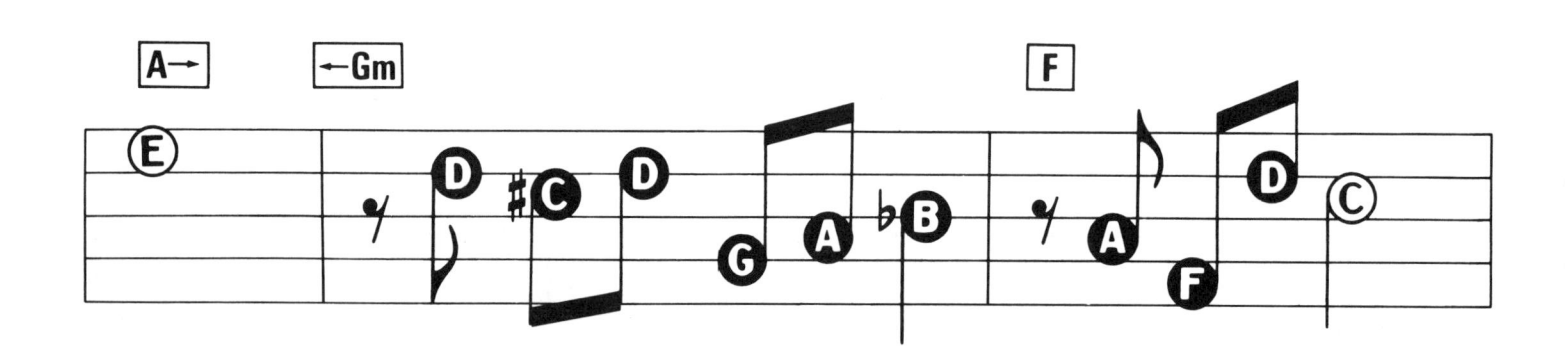

Registration 1

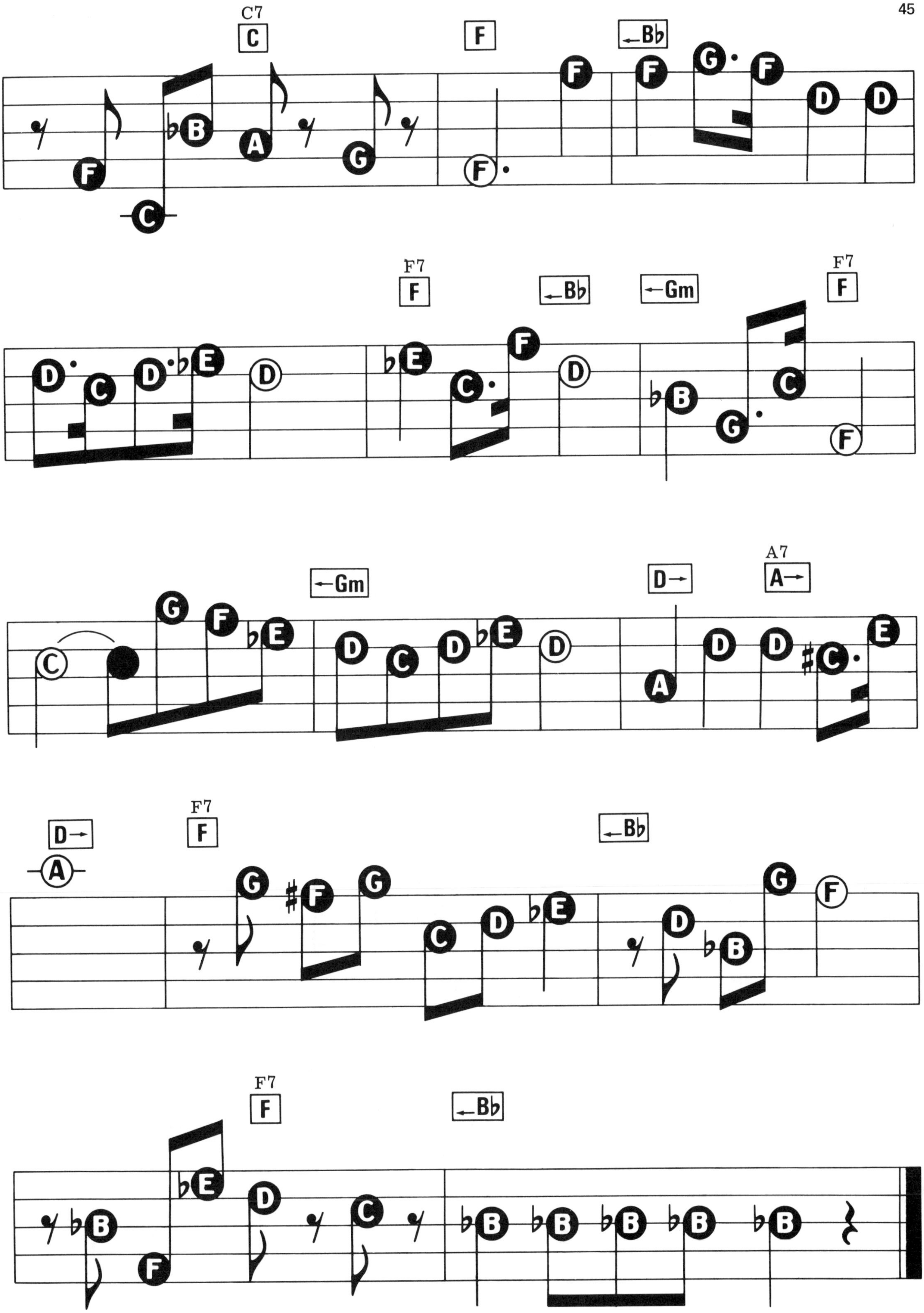
C7
C
F
←B♭
F7
F
←B♭
←Gm
F7
F
←Gm
D→
A7
A→
D→
F7
F
←B♭
F7
F
←B♭

Guitar Chord Chart

To use the E-Z Play TODAY Guitar Chord chart, simply find the **letter name** of the chord at the top of the chart, and the **kind of chord** (Major, Minor, etc.) in the column at the left. Read down and across to find the correct chord. Suggested fingering has been indicated, but feel free to use alternate fingering.

	C	D♭	D	E♭	E	F
MAJOR						
MINOR (m)						
7TH (7)						
MINOR 7TH (m7)						

	F#	**G**	**A♭**	**A**	**B♭**	**B**
MAJOR						
MINOR (m)						
7TH (7)						
MINOR 7TH (m7)						

Chord Speller Chart
of Standard Chord Positions

For those who play standard chord positions, all chords used in the E-Z Play TODAY music arrangements are shown here in their most commonly used chord positions. Suggested fingering is also indicated, but feel free to use alternate fingering.

CHORD FAMILY Abbrev.	MAJOR	MINOR (m)	7TH (7)	MINOR 7TH (m7)
C	5 2 1 G-C-E	5 2 1 G-C-Eb	5 3 2 1 G-Bb-C-E	5 3 2 1 G-Bb-C-Eb
Db	5 2 1 Ab-Db-F	5 2 1 Ab-Db-E	5 3 2 1 Ab-B-Db-F	5 3 2 1 Ab-B-Db-E
D	5 3 1 F#-A-D	5 2 1 A-D-F	5 3 2 1 F#-A-C-D	5 3 2 1 A-C-D-F
Eb	5 3 1 G-Bb-Eb	5 3 1 Gb-Bb-Eb	5 3 2 1 G-Bb-Db-Eb	5 3 2 1 Gb-Bb-Db-Eb
E	5 3 1 G#-B-E	5 3 1 G-B-E	5 3 2 1 G#-B-D-E	5 3 2 1 G-B-D-E
F	4 2 1 A-C-F	4 2 1 Ab-C-F	5 3 2 1 A-C-Eb-F	5 3 2 1 Ab-C-Eb-F
F#	4 2 1 F#-A#-C#	4 2 1 F#-A-C#	5 3 2 1 F#-A#-C#-E	5 3 2 1 F#-A-C#-E
G	5 3 1 G-B-D	5 3 1 G-Bb-D	5 3 2 1 G-B-D-F	5 3 2 1 G-Bb-D-F
Ab	4 2 1 Ab-C-Eb	4 2 1 Ab-B-Eb	5 3 2 1 Ab-C-Eb-Gb	5 3 2 1 Ab-B-Eb-Gb
A	4 2 1 A-C#-E	4 2 1 A-C-E	5 4 2 1 G-A-C#-E	5 4 2 1 G-A-C-E
Bb	4 2 1 Bb-D-F	4 2 1 Bb-Db-F	5 4 2 1 Ab-Bb-D-F	5 4 2 1 Ab-Bb-Db-F
B	5 2 1 F#-B-D#	5 2 1 F#-B-D	5 3 2 1 F#-A-B-D#	5 3 2 1 F#-A-B-D